1983

THE POETICS
OF DISGUISE

The Autobiography of the Work
in Homer, Dante, and Shakespeare

THE POETICS
OF DISGUISE

The Autobiography of the Work in
Homer, Dante, and Shakespeare

FRANCO FERRUCCI

Translated by Ann Dunnigan

Cornell University Press

ITHACA AND LONDON

First published 1980 by Cornell University Press.
Published in the United Kingdom by Cornell University Press Ltd.,
2-4 Brook Street, London W1Y 1AA.

Lines from Ezra Pound's *Pisan Cantos,* copyright 1948
by Ezra Pound, are reprinted by permission of
New Directions Publishing Corporation and Faber and Faber Ltd.

International Standard Book Number 0-8014-1262-5
Library of Congress Catalog Card Number 80-11242
Printed in the United States of America
Librarians: Library of Congress cataloging information
appears on the last page of the book.

Contents

	Introduction	11
1	The Shield of Achilleus	17
2	The Return of Odysseus	34
3	The Meeting with Geryon	66
4	The Two Poetics of the *Commedia*	103
5	*Macbeth* and the Imitation of Evil	125
6	Literary Models and the Autobiography of the Work	159
	Bibliography	169
	Index	177

Acknowledgments

Some of the material in this book was originally published in Italian in essay form; it has been thoroughly revised for the English version. All quotations from Homer are from Richmond Lattimore's translations, *The Iliad of Homer* (Chicago: University of Chicago Press, 1951, 1959) and *The Odyssey of Homer* (New York: Harper & Row, 1965, copyright © 1965, 1967 by Richmond Lattimore). The spelling of proper names follows Lattimore's. All quotations from *The Divine Comedy* are from the translation by Charles S. Singleton, Bollingen Series LXXX (Princeton, N.J.: Princeton University Press, *Inferno*, 1970, *Purgatorio*, 1973, *Paradiso*, 1975). All quotations from Shakespeare are from The Yale Shakespeare; *The Tragedy of Macbeth* has been edited for The Yale Shakespeare by Eugene M. Waith (New Haven: Yale University Press, revised edition, 1954).

I wish to express my gratitude to the Rutgers University Research Council for a grant that enabled me to complete the work. Very special thanks go to Ann Dunnigan, who has been much more than the translator of this book. Because of her constant and keen observation she can be considered the first editor of the manuscript and will remain one of its best readers.

Franco Ferrucci

New York, New York

THE POETICS
OF DISGUISE

The Autobiography of the Work
in Homer, Dante, and Shakespeare

Introduction

Each chapter of this book, except the last, is intended to be an autonomous inquiry into a single literary text. They are unified, however, by a similar critical approach. My interpretations begin from the observation that, in creative ventures, moments of grave crisis and perplexity are encountered, and threaten to stifle the entire work. Reality seems to resist the artistic endeavor to seize and represent it. This crucial point is metaphorized in the myth of the god Proteus who, through repeated metamorphoses, foils every attempt to capture him. In this duel the artist's victory requires not only genius but silence and cunning.

In my reading of each of the authors considered here I have encountered such moments, which operated as catalysts in my critical research: the description of Achilleus' shield in the *Iliad*, certain passages of the "Telemachy" and the end of the *Odyssey*, Dante's meeting with Geryon in the *Inferno*, and the first three scenes of Act IV in *Macbeth*. All of these are particularly suggestive sections of the masterpieces; there is a precarious balance between powerful tensions, between the requirements of expression and those of philosophical clarification. It is the artistic force of these episodes that originally caught my attention; I instinctively felt that their vibrations concealed an expressive drama that merited closer scrutiny.

Writers such as Homer, Dante, and Shakespeare, all profoundly marked by the classical ideal of expressive plenitude, would never have regarded the experience of a creative crisis as a sign of *noblesse d'esprit.* When the impasse is reached, they seek to disguise it. The phenomenon of disguise occurs at the most delicate moment of the author's work-in-progress, and the critic is privileged to discover its motivations and its structure. In fact, even when masked, the crisis manifests itself through signs and symptoms that are woven into the texture of the work, enhancing the richness and complexity of meaning. It is this weaving that I call the "autobiography of the work."

My use of the term "autobiography" does not imply any suggestion of the biographical experience of the artist himself. As will be observed in my hypothesis concerning Shakespeare, such experience may provide one of several motivations, but it should not be overemphasized by the critic. The autobiography of the work, in contradistinction to the autobiography of the author, is the reflection of the work upon itself at the crucial points of its becoming.

My approach entails a conception of the literary work as a living organism that must of necessity develop and flourish if is not to atrophy. This conception holds deep analogies with the organic theories of the artistic process that we find in the Romantic critics and poets, from Coleridge to Carlyle, from Herder to Goethe. (Some modern critics, among them Cleanth Brooks, have rediscovered and adopted such theories.) A similar idea is expressed with passionate vigor by Schopenhauer in chapter 49 of his major work, *The World as Will and Representation,* where he contrasts the works of the imitators with those of the creators. The former, "like parasitic plants, suck their nourishment from the works of others; and like polyps, take on the colour of their nourishment. Indeed, we could even carry the comparison farther, and assert that they are like machines which mince very fine and mix up what is put into them, but can never digest it, so that the constituent elements of others can always be found again, and picked out and separated from the mixture. Only the genius, on the other hand, is like the organic body that assimilates, transforms and produces." One difference between the romantic positions and mine is that the Romantics viewed the poet (the "genius") as the godlike or naturelike creator of the "work-plant," while I am tempted to suggest that the poet, not unlike a gardener, is only the necessary channel between nature and the work of art. My idea is not far from Heidegger's notion of *Schöpfung*, a creation that is also a "bringing to light," a drawing from a well that is sunk in the earth.

The role of the artist in this process, that of the indispensable and living link, is seen in the first stage of the work, its birth and growth. After the work has been completed, its rebirth and second flowering are repeated through the perusal of generations of readers. The critic can play a significant part in this process, for through his efforts the reader may be led back to a consideration of the original evolution of the text; thus the work is reanimated, given a fresh impetus, and its life cycle begins anew. An illustration of this concept of the work as an organism struggling to survive in time will be found in the last pages of the section on Dante.

The organic view of the work of art interests me for still another reason. The reader may wonder why, if one wishes to explain the relation between an author and his work, the writings in which the author himself directly addresses the question are not selected for investigation: in the case of Dante, the *Letter to Can Grande* and certain passages in the *Convivio*. And if the author has not left a specific poetics independent of the text under scrutiny, why should one not turn to those episodes in the work itself which explicitly deal with the phenomenon of artistic representation, such as Hamlet's advice to the actors? This is a decisive question to which an answer must be sought that will throw light on the methodology informing these chapters. The conception of the work as an organism provides the philosophical justification for the choices I have made.

If it is true that the genesis and development of a work of art follow intrinsic laws which the artist must perforce accept—and if it is true that the more fully he accepts them the more deeply he expresses himself—then the first conclusion to be drawn is that everything the author says that is not part of his own creative experience should be accepted with caution, not to say skepticism, whether stated before, after, or during the creative *épanouissement.* If the writer were able to elucidate with simplicity what he is doing, if it were really possible to translate into an expository language the root and flower of his inspiration, there would be no need for the work itself. Any deeply motivated work must necessarily be written in an idiosyncratic artistic language; it is the only mode in which a writer feels capable of expressing a particular idea of reality without distorting it. It is not possible to translate a discovery of the world into an explicit poetics without betraying the basic necessity that has guided the explorer.

At bottom, the problem derives from an unyielding presumption that the artist, close as he is to the origins of the work which we admire in its finished form, knows far more than we do about its significance and its implications. This is true, but in a more complex sense than might be thought. It seems to me that, in fact, the artist has but two certainties: one, the sensation he experiences of being on the right path; the other, the conviction that he has created something valid. The two certainties are in essence reduced to one, and in any case, are dictated by instinct rather than by rational considerations. The poetics of an author is the rationalization of his instinct, and the reader-critic should distrust it. The very closeness of the author to the work is, if anything, another element of the difficulty. He can tell us extraordinary things about the genesis of his work, but very little about the nature of his own creativitiy.

Many writers, quite realistically, have accepted this state of affairs, among the most recent the Italian poet Eugenio Montale. "The artist has no program," he writes in *Nel Nostro Tempo* "and no definable aim as a starting point. What moves him is the sense of a void to be filled, the presentiment of a form that he will recognize only when it has been attained." And further, "The degree of an artist's awareness is never absolute and is often entirely nebulous." His statements echo an observation made by Shelley: "The poet and the man are two different natures; though they exist together they may be unconscious of each other, and incapable of deciding upon each other's powers and efforts by any reflex act." When Wayne C. Booth declares that the "implied author is always distinct from the real man," he says basically the same thing, although for different purposes and in a different context. At the opposite pole one might cite Zola and the poetics of naturalism, Joyce and the poetics of epiphany, Pirandello and the poetics of the conflict between life and form. I believe that any critic who penetrates the works of these authors will feel the need to disregard such theories, which the artist offers as a guided tour into the heart of a work.

One should view with the same distrust, and for the same reasons, those passages of undisguised poetics which an author introduces into his work. They often produce the effect of a botanical label attached to a plant: one feels impelled to remove it, the better to enjoy and understand the plant. But the crucial moments, the moments when the author commingles an unconscious definition of his work with its creation, are rare, unexpected, and untranslatable into a language other than that of art itself, and the critic, by the mere fact of being outside the creation, is probably in a better position than the author to identify them.

What instruments will the critic use in his research? What will serve as his stethoscope, his electric eye, his gauge of creative energy? In a period when an ideological faith in the methodology of literary interpretation reigns supreme, my reply to these questions may prove disappointing. It is my conviction that all, or much, depends on his humility before the work under scrutiny—the same humility the artist feels before his inspiration. The interpretive possibilities are infinite, and every interpretation is justified by its particular cogency rather than by its reliance on a methodology that is deemed appropriate. The more objective the critic, the more he will realize the ineluctable subjectivity of his interpretive choices.

Of course it is possible to offer an interpretation of the work of art in which the author's autobiography serves as a propedeutic instrument. But even if Shakespeare's feelings toward King James were other than those I ascribe to him in the chapter on *Macbeth*, that would not alter the fact that all his plays written during the same period show profound indications of crisis and change, whose evidence could be perceived in the writing though we knew no more of the author than we know of Homer. What is important is that the two phenomena (the necessity of disguising the impasse in the representation of reality, and the need to reveal the crisis in oblique and symbolic form) are constantly united in the artistic experience of each author considered here. One can retain this relation as a major aspect of literary creation, as I indicate in the last chapter.

In the course of writing this book I have come to realize how important for each of the authors discussed is his relation to his tradition and to an esteemed literary model. I focus on this matter in my conclusion.

1

The Shield of Achilleus

After the death of Patroklos, Achilleus requires new armor, and his mother, the goddess Thetis, appeals to Hephaistos to forge it for her son. When the hero is about to receive the god's handiwork, Homer gives a singularly detailed description of the shield. This somewhat lengthy delineation has impressed many readers as little more than a bravura passage. A closer reading, however, suggests a further interpretation: the shield is a mirror of a new and final stage of consciousness attained by Achilleus. If this is so, the passage represents the primal example of the autobiography of a work, the first instance of a work of art speculating about itself, and the description of the shield is a focal point of the poem.

If we consider the comprehensive meaning of the *Iliad*, we may see the poem not only as an account of the epic conflict between two formidable armies, as we have been taught to read it, but as the first attempt to give a total representation of human life and the growth of human awareness. The first aspect is embodied in the image of the siege, the second in the character of Achilleus.

At the very inception of Western literature, the Homeric poems offered the two models for the representation of reality which were to be fundamental to the history of narrative forms: the *Iliad*, model of the siege, and the *Odyssey*, model of the return. Although the ground had been prepared by countless oral legends, Mediterranean and Eastern, the *Iliad*, the first book, appears to posterity as self-immured, with illusory phantoms of primeval memory hovering at its doors. The book, which portrays a siege, is itself a literary fortress.

The siege is the first narrative model of our literary tradition. It is spatially static, and its structure can be compared to a circle. The action gravitates toward a point of density both physical and metaphysical: the naught, the all, the point of equilibrium between two forces which stand in opposition to each other in a stalemate. In the *Iliad*, the two forces are called Achaians and Trojans. The extent of the Trojan War exceeds the limits of the work, as Homer deals with neither its beginning nor its end. Troy, its thousand-year-old walls besieged by external forces, is the *encircled* place. Its conquest is to be its destruction.

The events prior to the conflict, recalled only fleetingly, as in a dream, are exceedingly remote; the characters of the poem live almost devoid of memory, locked in a present that absorbs and engulfs them. When, from the tower parapet of Troy, Helen points out to Priam the Achaian heroes Agamemnon, Odysseus, and Aias, one wonders why the old king has not, in nine years, learned to recognize them. The procession of Greek warriors at the end of Book II serves more as a cognitive survey than a parade drill. It is the moment when the adversaries appraise one another with renewed interest because of occurrences at the beginning of the epic, which are of great symbolic significance: the plague and the subsequent wrath of Achilleus.

To understand better the metaphorical aspect of the work, one must first be convinced that the *Iliad* as a whole, presenting life in its fundamental constituents, is one great metaphor. The Trojan War (whose origins are almost mythical in the memories of the besiegers) spans the lifetime of mankind, including its prehistory. The moment the story begins, symbolically one enters human history, and thus the consciousness of one's own condition. Between the wrath of Achilleus and the death of Hektor, Homer depicts civilization's history from its origin to the point at which he himself has arrived—only yesterday in relationship to today; consequently we find his conclusions valid for us as well.

That Homer begins his narrative toward the end of the siege reveals one of his most profound insights: having entered history, man has remaining to him but a fraction of the amount of time he has already lived, since civilization is but the end of a long development. The real end, the conquest of Troy, is not described, because it represents the end of human history, which is yet to be experienced. But the eventual outcome is beyond doubt: that Troy's fate is sealed, that its walls will fall, is reiterated like a ceaseless refrain by both gods and warriors. If the beginning of the war is uncertain, and vertiginously remote, its termination is never in doubt. It is the common belief that the force of gravity drawing the Achaians toward the center of the circle is ineluctable: at the end lies death, the only certain end for every individual and collective experience.

In this simple yet ingenious model (which is also a time-space structure), the first event recounted is that of the plague. We view the event with a certain emotion, for it is the beginning not only of the poem but of all Western literature as well. We know, too, that plague is to be of momentous significance both as a narrative theme and as a symbol from Thucydides to Lucretius, from Boccaccio to Defoe, from Manzoni to Camus. Already in the *Iliad* it is a portentous and mysteriously decisive event.

To pursue our schema of interpretation: the plague surges during the time of the advent of consciousness in the human world, and just as every advance in understanding inevitably brings with it the realization that life is tragic and that human problems have no real solutions, this consciousness is experienced as mental anguish and disease. So, in the Homeric dawn of creation, the light of reason is manifested as a chronic and incurable disease, what Freud was later to define as the discontent of civilization.

Several centuries after the *Iliad,* the Homeric note is sounded in *Oedipus the King.* Here too a plague signals the advent of a consciousness that develops from a guilty conscience; and here too it is a matter of identifying the culprit in the person of a leader. But in Sophocles' tragedy the action must lead beyond mere recognition of the guilt, to its exemplary punishment; hence the ascendancy of the chorus, led by professional moralists and representing the consciousness of the group. For Sophocles, to become conscious means to recognize one's guilt — a conclusion which, in Occidental tradition, derives from a spirit that will find its most dynamic expression in the Old Testament. Sophocles' tragedy is dominated by a sacerdotal spirit. The real guilt is that of not feeling guilty and purification is accompanied by humiliation and exemplified in expiation; only at this price will the hero recover the noble stature of a great human model. In tragedy the gods are masks that reaffirm the authority of the priests and legitimize the tyranny of terror.

Homer's view is quite different: for him, becoming conscious means recognizing not one's guilt but one's humanity. The concept of hubris, common to the Book of Genesis and Greek tragedy alike, would have been incomprehensible to him: the strife between men and gods has neither moral nor metaphysical connotations; the two worlds are so close they almost touch; in fact, one has only to be beautiful to be "godlike." The awesome concept of sin has yet to be formulated in his universe: not to feel guilty means not to be guilty; it is remorse that generates guilt, not vice versa. Instead of feeling guilty (as the priests would like him to do) Achilleus begins to realize that the situation involves every participant in the war and that there is no solution. His anger over the loss of Briseis is sincere but also contains a distinct implication of awareness of the common fate.

Let us review the reasons for the war. Conquest and pillage are major motives, but would hardly have sufficed without the dream of retrieving Helen. When she appears on the battlements of Troy, the reaction of the besieged is revealing. No one, apart from Hektor, thinks of casting blame on her. With her irresistible beauty, she embodies the dream of happiness pursued by all the participants, besieged and besiegers alike. Helen poses a question of life or death; to give her up is unthinkable, and to relinquish the idea of recapturing her equally so. Helen is the common objective, and through her we perceive the significance of the theme of abduction and siege. Ever since the commencement of man's existence (at the beginning of the Trojan War, according to our schema of interpretation), something essential has been wrested from him and carried off. In his struggle to the death to regain possession of his lost property, he has gone to any lengths to retrieve it, even to the extent of setting in motion the outrageous mechanism called civilization. But he has inevitably ended by recognizing himself in the enemy he confronts.

During all the years he has blindly battled, the warrior has concealed from himself the most difficult truth—that the struggle is with himself. The circle of Troy, in whose center stands Helen, is the space around which the besieger accomplishes his own destruction together with that of the besieged; the circle is an insidious field of conquest in which both hunter and prey are trapped. If, at the beginning of the poem, the plague represents the pernicious wave of self-consciousness that gives rise to the crisis in the Achaian camp, the first to suffer the consequences of the awareness is Achilleus. It is characteristic of every advance of self-consciousness that the individual first takes cognizance of his own situation; here the awareness occurs at the moment when Achilleus finds himself deprived of Briseis. One understands then why he gives such importance to his female booty. This Helen for whom all are fighting, this center they all seek to reach, becomes in Achilleus' eyes a bitter mockery, a mere mirage. If Briseis is taken from him, what is the meaning of the common endeavor to obtain Helen? As a result of a personal conflict, the truth, till then concealed from all of them, flashes across his mind: blood is being shed in the pursuit of a chimera of happiness which, day after day, is paid for with sacrifices for which there is no recompense.

Yet the fact remains that turning back is impossible. Though sometimes spoken of during Achilleus' withdrawal among his ships, it never becomes a real possibility. From the time this fragile giant—the first problematic hero in Western literature —assumes the enormous burden of consciousness, he alone has the means to escape the destructive mechansim and renounce the war. But all he does is take refuge in his tent. His is not a return, but rather the first experience of what the Stoic sages will later term *epoché*. Achilleus quits the battle and places himself outside life. When Odysseus and Aias come to him as emissaries from Agamemnon, they do not find a wrathful, overwrought man but a gracious host who invites them to sit down, serves them supper, and then courteously rejects their entreaties. When his visitors have departed, he and Patroklos, of one accord, go off to bed, each with a woman, taking Helen in their own way, as it were, without further struggle. This solution has been anticipated in Book 1 of the poem when, after a turbulent day, the gods assemble for a banquet enlivened by Olympian laughter at Hephaistos' jests.

Even in his isolated state, two certainties remain with Achilleus: Troy is destined to fall, and he will meet his death in the course of the siege. His own death and that of the enemy are one. The striving for individuation leads him to discover among the Trojan host his mirror image, Hektor. To kill him will be the culmination of a mirror war in which every warrior pursues his own image. And though this is as true for the others as for him, they do not act consciously. Menelaos confronts Paris, disarms and drags him in the dust, till Aphrodite comes to his rescue and transports him to Helen's perfumed bed, while his rival continues to range the battlefield. In the same way, Diomedes repeatedly tries to kill Aineias, who is first protected by Aphrodite, then by Apollo. Not one of the great heroes is killed in battle; even the single combat between Hektor and Aias, which should have decided the outcome of the war, ends without victory on either side and with an exchange of gifts and expressions of esteem. In the heat of battle, when anyone comes close to killing his mirror image, the gods intervene to protect the vanquished one. The moment there is a respite, the heroes arrange a separate truce, a personal armistice, as do Glaukos and Diomedes, and then automatically return to massacring minor figures.

The entire Trojan War is one long temporization. Everyone seeks to defer the inevitable event that will upset the delicate balance of the siege, a condition maintained by a system of weights and counterweights. The present-day human world of consciousness and history knows that its survival hangs by a thread. It also knows that it is living a prolonged paradox: man is driven to attack by an immemorial habit that confounds his past with that of the beasts. In the *Iliad,* the repeated comparisons of men to wild animals highlight this meaning. The force of inertia inscribed in the animal heredity of the species impels man toward the center of the circle, toward his own end. Millenniums of prehistory (years of siege, according to Homer's symbolic contraction) are decisive, bearing down on him and imposing a direction and a pattern of behavior. The only guarantee of survival is in maintaining a stalemate whereby man is blocked without being immobilized. The Trojan War is a series of inconclusive battles that fail to advance the conflict, a massacre of pawns that leaves intact the major pieces on the tottering chessboard.

Achilleus' wrath is manifested on two different occasions: when he withdraws from the war, and when he returns to it. The first temporarily upsets the balance of power; the second radically accelerates the fall of Troy. Interpreted symbolically, both stages are necessary and in no way contradictory. In the first instance, he realizes that the struggle is *futile,* and in the second, that it is *inevitable.* One has only to observe what happens when the hero retires from the scene of battle: no sooner has the pressure of the assault diminished than the besieged Trojans counterattack. A battlefield is established between Troy and the seacoast, where several warrior heroes confront each other—Diomedes and the two Aiantes on one side and Hektor on the other. Leading his men toward the Achaian ships, Hektor encounters the unexpected: the Greeks have built a wall around the ships, and now the siege is duplicated in reverse. As an immutable construct of human behavior, siege is thus inevitable; if one side does not resort to it, the other will. But the difference is that the Achaians have proceeded slowly toward the center of the circle, while Hektor, in his counterattack, comes very close to victory. In order to avert the collapse of their last defenses, the Greeks will require the return of Achilleus to the war.

All this means that the course of human life is irreversible, for if it were not, the precarious balance of opposites would be destroyed. In short, it is impossible to besiege the besieger, except for an illusory moment; although the two armies mirror each other, they are not permitted to alter the direction of the action. Man knows that death awaits him, but cannot revert to youth; the earth rushes headlong toward destruction, but still rotates in the same direction. All this is what Homer shows us. There is no way to evade the siege, or even to reverse it.

The figure of Hektor is analogous to that of Achilleus. The birth of consciousness occurs in the besieged as well as in the besieger: Hektor too knows that he must die before Troy is conquered, and he too resolves to oppose the mechanism. But although Achilleus chooses to abstain from the action, Hektor, because of his contrary position, seeks to reverse it.

Hektor's fury has a suicidal impetus, which is understandable when one considers that he is engaged in a desperate struggle to overcome destiny. Let us refer to Book XII, which immediately precedes the assault on the walls built by the Greeks to block access to their ships. After a prolonged battle, the outcome is still uncertain:

> ... as two men with measuring ropes in their hands fight
> bitterly
> about a boundary line at the meeting place of two
> cornfields,

and the two of them fight in the strait place over the rights
      of division,
so the battlements held these armies apart.

                    [XII, 421–424]

.   .   .   .   .

Everywhere the battlements and the bastions were awash
with men's blood shed from both sides, Achaian and
      Trojan.
But even so they could not drive panic among the Achaians,
but held evenly as the scales which a careful widow
holds, taking it by the balance beam, and weighs her wool
      evenly
at either end, working to win a pitiful wage for her children:
so the battles fought by both sides were pulled fast and even.

                    [XII, 430–436]

These comparisons signal the recovery of an equilibrium that
has been at the point of dissolution, and the similes elaborating
visions of equilibrium expand the hope of making it endure.
Even after Hektor has shattered the fortification by casting a
stone that seems to break a natural as well as a human barrier,
the poet attempts to create a similar moment. The Greeks or-
ganize another defense; when the Trojans attack, they resist
without repulsing them, and a new stage is evoked.

as a chalkline straightens the cutting of a ship's timber
in the hands of an expert carpenter, who by Athene's
inspiration is well versed in all his craft's subtlety,
so the battles fought by both sides were pulled fast and even.

                    [XV, 410–413]

The references are to a completely human world; for once,
the warriors are not compared to ravening lions; vivid, and

with a subtle flavor of paradox, the similes conjure up a world of work. In the first, we see two men with measuring ropes in their hands quarreling over the allotment of two equal parts of land. Here Homer suggests the situation of the warriors: in order to survive, both sides must perpetuate an equilibrium that is possible only in conflict. The unconscious ideal would be one of waging war without conquest to attain those equal parts, to reach the equilibrium toward which they are striving in vain. In the second, we see a woman weighing her wool evenly, careful to rob no one, and all for a meager recompense. Is such an effort (life) worth such a compensation (suffering)?

At the moment of the final encounter between the two heroes, the image of the scales will again be evoked, *a parte deorum:*

> then the Father balanced his golden scales, and in them
> he set two fateful portions of death, which lays men
> > prostrate,
> one for Achilleus, and one for Hektor, breaker of horses,
> and balanced it by the middle; and Hektor's death-day was
> > heavier
> and dragged downward toward death.
>
> > > [XXII, 209–213]

After killing Patroklos, Hektor puts on the armor that Achilleus lent his friend, and again flies to the battlefield. Zeus, in the clouds above, takes pity on the hero rushing to meet his death; at a sign from the god, the armor fits itself so perfectly to Hektor's body that his strength is like that of Ares himself. With fierce cries, the hero goes straight toward the battle as all look on in dismay

> ... He went onward calling in a great voice
> to his renowned companions in arms, and figured before
> > them
> flaming in the battle gear of great-hearted Pelion.
>
> > > [XVII, 212–214]

The passage is charged with meaning: Hektor *is* Achilleus. Now that he wears Achilleus' armor, the similarity between their destinies is made manifest and will be made still clearer in the episode of the final duel between them (Book xii). After the two heroes have met and exchanged their rancorous threats, Hektor is overcome by an unexpected terror which compels him to flee, and three times he races round the walls of Troy, like one who besieges a city and fails in his attempts to enter it; each time he is forestalled by Achilleus, who momentarily becomes Troy's defender. In this exchange of roles, the two men recognize themselves as mirror images of each other; their victory does not depend on themselves, for it is inscribed in the book of destiny. The immutable image is that of the siege.

And, in fact, around the body of Patroklos a battle had raged, which was yet another attempt to reconstruct a circle of siege.

> For Aias ranged their whole extent with his numerous
>   orders,
> and would not let any man give back from the body, nor let
>   one
> go out and fight by himself far in front of the other
>   Achaians,
> but made them stand hard and fast about him and fight at
>   close quarters.
> Such were the orders of gigantic Aias.
>
> [xvii, 356-350]

The contest is isolated from the rest of the world.

> So they fought on in the likeness of fire, nor would you have
>   thought
> the sun was still secure in his place in the sky, nor the moon,
>   since
> the mist was closed over all that part of the fight where the
>   bravest

27

> stood about Patroklos, the fallen son of Menoitios.
>
> [XVII, 366-369]

Enveloped in clouds of dust, the hallucinating warriors pursue a dream of stasis. Later, Achilleus' horses "standing apart from the battle wept."

> ... but still as stands a grave monument which is set over the mounded tomb of a dead man or lady, they stood there holding motionless in its place the fair-wrought chariot, leaning their heads along the ground.
>
> [XVII, 434-437]

The ideal then is to remain in an adamant immobility that wards off the specter of the end.

These battle descriptions show the *Iliad* as a poem of space. Here the struggle for survival is pursued in spatial terms, while in the *Odyssey* it is enacted in temporal sequences. There is a great physical freedom in the *Odyssey,* largely illusory but of definite descriptive efficacy; the hero sails from coast to coast across the open sea and the scene of the action changes frantically. There are also states of captivity (on the islands of Kalypso, Polyphemos and Circe), insofar as every restriction of movement is felt as an act of violation and of physical constraint. No such situation appears in the *Iliad.* If one were to gauge the size of the theater of war, it would be evident that for nine years the warriors are confined to a ribbon of land between Troy's walls and the sea—land on which a man can hardly move without colliding with an enemy. The siege, for both besieger and besieged, is the torment induced by being restricted to a narrow space. Just as Odysseus combats passing time in the *Odyssey* (every moment lost is like a wound that delays the return), so the heroes of the *Iliad* fight for every inch of ground "as two men ... fight bitterly about a boundary line" (XII, 421-422). The fear in the *Iliad,* as in a game of chess, is that of losing ground.

When Achilleus' terrible cry shatters the equilibrium between opposite forces that is created around the corpse of Patroklos, in vain does Thetis remind her son that he is doomed to die soon after Hektor. The hero is eager to return to the battle, but he must have new armor. Here we come to the description of his portentous shield.

Only to the shield does Homer devote meticulous attention; the other arms are given a rather summary description. A weapon of defense, not of attack, it is interposed between Achilleus and the world, which it reflects even as it protects him from it. Round in shape, encircled by a representation of the Ocean River, which is also the outer boundary of the earth, and with the sun, the moon, and all the constellations depicted in the center, it is a compendium of the cosmos. If the shield represents Achilleus' consciousness, the vision of the cosmos is enclosed in the heart of consciousness as the stone in the fruit. And if Achilleus wishes to renounce his isolation and return to life and to the war, he will have to avail himself of the protective shield in order to carry with him the image of life while living it. Art, of which the shield is a definitive example, is entrusted with expressing reality while at the same time functioning as a defense against its threat.

The *Iliad* presents a world without bards or poets: the "youth with a singing lyre" whom we find in the description of Achilleus' shield is, according to Homer scholars, a later interpolation. This is a world embellished by music and dance, by spectacles in which speech is linked to movement, as in the exposition of a mobile painting. But the path to poetry is marked; if the professional poet or bard is lacking, poetry itself is being born. In the midst of a rustic festival we see a youth who sings, while other youths follow his song in dance. We are not far from a time foreseen by Helen in her encounter with Hektor:

> us two, on whom Zeus set a vile destiny, so that hereafter
> we shall be made into things of song for the men
>   of the future.

[VI, 357-358]

29

Helen foresees a time when the *Iliad* will be written, this poem
that depicts a world without literature, as is proper for a first
book which must define once and for all the limits of the written
word. The birth of art is entrusted to Hephaistos, *faber et artifex*,
the deformed god who resembles those stricken men who would
return to life.

The vision of the cosmos, which is in the center of the shield, is
expanded in a delineation of scenes of everyday life. Here are
two cities, as seen by the man who has surmounted voluntary
exile and decided to re-enter the struggle: cities seen as mirror
reflections of each other, one at peace and one at war. The
peaceful city is celebrating nuptial feasts with dance and song,
but elsewhere, in the tumult of the marketplace, two men are
disputing the blood price of a man who has been killed.

In his portrayal of these two cities, Homer pictures the good
things of life: all that man can fabricate and enjoy while awaiting
disaster. There is the rural imagery of reaping, grape harvest-
ing, and grazing, with song and dance accompanying the pas-
toral rites. Two lions are attacking a bull, but on the whole, the
effect is one of restful and luxuriant beauty. Where in the poem
is this beatific life concealed if the entire work shows us only the
violence of life surrounding Troy? The peaceful scenes unfold
like clouds rising from the souls of the warriors: dreams and
images of a happy life, fragments of which reach them in
moments of respite. Dreams even assume names and pass
among men in the guise of gods whose companionship they
enjoy. It is the nature of wisdom to know how to live with illusions, and of despair to have no illusions. On Achilleus' shield,
the hero who is required to return to the struggle must keep
faith with the notion of a happy life.

This is the significance of Achilleus' shield. As an image of the
hero's consciousness, it reflects the cosmos while representing it,
and is thus the first symbolic image of art's capacity to function
as a stereoscope. Characteristically, Homer attributes the very
human activity of art to a god. The poet combines maternal

intervention (Thetis) with a craftsman's industry (Hephaistos); the latter surmounts his physical defects through his skill as an artificer. Art is a remedy for physical and spiritual suffering, and at the point of consciousness and lucidity to which Achilleus is thrust, art is the shield that defends man from the violence of life. Knowledge, defender, and instrument of war, the shield allows Achilleus to face life (war) without being overcome by it. Yet this protection does not delude him about his own fate.

Thus, the wrath of Achilleus which defines the human story is the shaft of light that conscience casts upon nature's path. The idea of living in a twilight that succeeds the dawn of the gods and the noonday of men is found even in the first book. It is a book born to have no sequel, for it has said everything. As a similar situation recurs in every great book, the paradox of writing is continually magnified. The first model of reality has been created, the first work contains its own interpretation; art has already the power to formulate art. The cosmos contains the poem, in which resides the shield—the shield that reflects the universe. The poem becomes an image of the cosmos so complete as to discourage any attempt to compete with it. The first book aspires to be the book of human history.

No one, perhaps, not even in that remote time when the limits of memory were uncertain, could have supposed that Homer would have been the first to attempt to challenge such a book by writing another. One must recognize the difficulty of the venture: the *Iliad* is presented as a compact block, a veritable literary fortress all but impossible to storm. The concept of life that emanates from this citadel is complete. Human memory traces in the action of the *Iliad* an event without memory; even when Glaukos and Diomedes speak of their ancestors, they do not seem to be remembering so much as reciting a genealogy that unfolds in the present like an ancient scroll. But if the work has no memory that we can decipher, what is the act of writing? It is already a remembering. Homer has awakened and recounts: the artist cannot help turning to the past, his only material. While we are remembering his work, he is recalling the facts of the poem; Homer is not the thing recounted but he who recounts. Without him memory would be lost.

This emerges at the end of the *Iliad*. If Achilleus also represents the dawning artistic consciousness, it is clear that the only page of true memory in the entire poem is the one that describes his meeting with Priam. The period of the bards, those professionals of remembering, is approaching. The link with the *Odyssey*, this poem of memory, is marked: the closed work, by definition, has exposed a breach in its own mechanism of defense. To continue the *Iliad* would be tantamount to an admission that not all has been said that can be said, and even to a refutation of it conclusions. Consequently, the idea of the return arises as a alternative to the theme of the siege. The author of the *Iliad* ha perhaps grown several years, or decades, older, or else one generation has replaced another. The conception of another grea narrative poem, the *Odyssey*, is born of the need to oppose one model of reality to another. It is not a question of the concept of reality, because the *Odyssey* basically accepts the conclusions of the *Iliad*, but rather of seeing whether it is possible, if only as a gamble, to challenge the greatness of that first artistic event.

The *Odyssey* tells of Odysseus' device of the wooden horse, an artifice that serves to open the inevitable breach in Troy's defense. That it should be Odysseus, the protagonist of the new poem, who devises this expedient, seems to imply a meaning that defines the relation between the two works. The artistic structure of the siege collapses as a result of a stratagem and a deception, and thus the representation of the return can begin, the illusion so long negated by the philosophical essence of the *Iliad*. In the *Odyssey* we are in the realm of deception and mystification, and Odysseus is the new hero of the challenge of the return. To return home is equivalent to recapturing lost happiness, which everyone vainly pursues in seeking to recapture Helen.

The representation of reality is the greatest claim to glory of a work of art. But when it is later challenged by another work, reality temporarily becomes a battlefield where two models con-

front each other. If the *Iliad* is right, Odysseus should not return; but once it is decided to portray his return, an effort is
initiated to bend reality to fit artistic ends. Thus begins the
course of literature, which arises in reaction to other works as
well as to the real world. But the birth of poetry will only confirm
the words of Helen to Hektor, the same words that will be spoken by King Alkinoös at the royal palace of the Phaiakians when
he tries to persuade Odysseus to speak:

> ... The gods did this, and spun the destruction
> of peoples, for the sake of the singing of men hereafter.
>
> [*Odyssey*, VIII, 579–580]

2

The Return of Odysseus

There is an episode in Book IV of the *Odyssey* in which Telemachos solicits news of his father, and Menelaos gratifies him by
relating the story of his encounter with Proteus, the god of perpetual metamorphoses. This divine personage does not appear
in the *Iliad,* but his presence in the *Odyssey* is fully justified: in
effect, he epitomizes the spirit of the whole work. Proteus knows
the truth of every event and of every individual destiny—that of
Aias, Agamemnon, and Odysseus. He is not disposed to reveal
his knowledge, however, and Menelaos is obliged to enter into a
violent struggle with him to compel him to speak. In the course
of the conflict, Proteus successively transforms himself into a
tree, water, fire, and wild beasts, but Menelaos refuses to relinquish his hold on him, and in the end the god is forced to admit
defeat. He then divulges to Menelaos that Odysseus is held captive on Kalypso's island and that he is destined to return.

This episode is the culminating point of the "Telemachy," the
early section of the poem which is the prelude to Odysseus'
entrance on the scene. It focuses on the figure of the hero's
young son and is of singular interest not only as a narrative but
as a metaphor: as an autobiography of the artistic process itself.
One instance of such autobiography was, as we saw, the description of Achilleus' shield, a metaphor for the emergence of the

artistic phenomenon at the heart of civilization. The *Odyssey* multiplies this type of connotation, a characteristic of its spirit, which is considerably more reflective and intellectual than that of the *Iliad*. The more mature and conscious art becomes, the more it questions itself and its own procedures; it travels, so to say, accompanied by its own shadow. Thus, for both reader and critic there evolves the possibility of a double register of reading, more fascinating for being unexpected.

The climax of the encounter with Proteus has been carefully prepared by the preceding events. The "Telemachy" can be read on more than one level. Literally, it tells of Telemachos' sorrow and his years of waiting in a house that has been invaded by the Suitors. On the psychological level of character interpretation, Telemachos' waiting for Odysseus reflects his desire for maturity, the need to change from an adolescent to an adult ready for action. On the level of the autobiography of the work, the waiting for Odysseus, the intense longing for him to appear, betrays the anxiety that accompanies Homer's new poetic inspiration. To wonder whether Odysseus will return is tantamount to asking, Can the *Odyssey* take place?

At the opening of the poem, once again Homer begins with the Immortals, directors committed to an action that calls for staging, backdrops, callboys, and prompters. The gods know what men dimly desire; their words anticipate what men are to experience. On Olympos, the action of the *Odyssey,* swirls like a fantastic primordial nucleus, an inspiration that will be realized only when it is manifested on earth. Athene, serving as intermediary between one episode and the next, flies to Ithaka; it is the moment in which, for the first time, the dream tries to materialize. Not by chance does the goddess, disguised as an unknown guest, hasten toward Telemachos like the beam of a spotlight picking out the first tremulous actor. Timid and irresolute, Telemachos grieves over all that has happened without knowing how to resolve his problems. In the hall where the Suitors banquet, the bard Phemios sings of the great heroes. It is an atmosphere Schiller would term "sentimental," that is, charged with memories and nostalgia; indeed, as we shall see repeatedly, memory is the dimension discovered by the new poem.

The *Odyssey* lives under the weight of an event at once mysterious and tangible. All the characters in the poem know of the existence of the *Iliad;* they know it not because they have read the book, which for them does not yet exist, but because the author knows it and projects his experience of it into his new creation. The relation of the *Odyssey* to the past is no longer conveyed solely by means of the immemorial oral tradition, which is destined to be absorbed, but through the already existing written book, always in mind but never named; thus the author and his characters are imbued with the past. When Odysseus goes to the palace of Alkinoös, at first he refuses to give his name; but when the bard enters and sings of Odysseus' exploits, the unknown hero draws his mantle over his head to conceal his tears. In the end, he decides to reveal his identity and to relate his story from the time Troy fell, including his return following the siege. "I will tell you of my voyage home with its many troubles" (IX, 37–38). The nostalgic and "sentimental" dimension created by the bard's song is essential to an understanding of the climate of the new work.

According to the spirit of the *Iliad, the return would not be possible.* The fate of the survivors of Troy conjured up by the bard's song seems in large part to confirm this. Some, like Aias, are lost on the way back and die; others, like Agamemnon, reach home and are murdered. The disastrous fate of the defeated Trojans is prolonged in the individual tragedies of the victorious besiegers. To believe in a return without tragedy is to reverse the conclusions of the great book, to negate the fate of a common destruction. In the beginning of the *Odyssey,* Telemachos is both victim and spectator of a situation typifying human existence, a kind of situation already immortalized in the *Iliad:* a futile siege, this time a siege of the Suitors, enacted in his own house with his mother, Penelope, as its object. The drama of the youthful hero, of which Telemachos is the notable archetype, is all here; looking about him he discovers what the songs of heroes have taught him to see, but he sees it as impoverished and debased. Everything savors of decadence: the feasts have become carouses; the great battles, the brawling of arrogant drunkards. A "sentimental" world is one in which a person is convinced that there has been a better world and that the present one is but an ugly counterfeit; hence the need to evoke the past through the bards' songs and to shed tears of dim hope.

When Athene, in the guise of a guest, announces to him the possibility of Odysseus' return, Telemachos replies:

> ... I will accurately answer all that you ask me.
> My mother says indeed I am his. I for my part
> do not know. Nobody really knows his own father.
>
> [I, 214–216]

Athene has already told him he resembles Odysseus; Menelaos will later also say so. In making Odysseus and Telemachos mirror images, Homer repeats the device he used in the *Iliad* with Hektor and Achilles; but here, in the *Odyssey,* the new dimensions of time and memory create a mirroring of two generations, of two individuals separated by time and space. On the psychological level, the return of Odysseus will mean for Telemachos the possibility of attaining manhood, of ripening the seeds of resemblance to his legendary father. He must prove himself the son of Odysseus, just as Odysseus will continually have to prove that he is Odysseus. The *Odyssey* is assuredly one of the works in which the problem of identity is most acutely and profoundly perceived. A doubt is often voiced by its characters: And what if I am not what I am? And what if this guest is other than he seems? The spirit of Proteus runs through the entire poem. There is a repeated question: Speak, stranger, tell me who you are; have you ever encountered my father? And Athene replies to Telemachos in a way very characteristic of the *Odyssey* by telling him a truth (Odysseus is alive and will return) tempered with deceit concerning her own ostensible activity as a

37

merchant. Moreover, she has disguised herself with the facility for impersonation natural to the gods. This is but the first of an infinite number of stratagems found throughout the poem. Simulation and dissimulation become the primary techniques of human intercourse. On presenting himself to Nestor and Menelaos, Telemachos refuses to reveal his name; Odysseus will often do the same.

In the beginning, Odysseus' return seems to depend above all on the intensity with which Telemachos is capable of desiring it. The occasion will signify a maturation, the passage from adolescence to manhood; if Telemachos has confidence in his own metamorphosis, the hero can appear. Remember that Telemachos and Odysseus will return to Ithaka simultaneously, landing at different points on the coast; the mirroring of their destinies could not be more vividly expressed. But on the level of the autobiography of the work, the entire evolution of Telemachos appears to symbolize the question put to the artist by himself: am I equal to the challenge of the *Iliad*? Telemachos is like the unsure poet (Homer) overwhelmed by the bards' songs: only when he believes in the return of Odysseus will the *Odyssey* be born. Hear my counsel, says Athene to Telemachos: Put out to sea; go question those who have happily returned, Nestor and Menelaos. That is to say, enter into reality; inquire of life whether the return is possible. Only the returned heroes can give you news of your father. Telemachos' journey represents the confrontation with external reality, the quest for a new representative model as a counterpart to that of the siege.

The theme Nestor expounds at length to the young hero who comes to him is that of Agamemnon's doom. Athene has already spoken of it, and Menelaos will further expatiate on his brother's tragic end. The subject recurs with such insistency that one can scarcely doubt that Telemachos is to be offered an alternative destiny: if he is capable of believing in the return, Odysseus will come home; if, along with his mother, he yields to the Suitors, a fate as black as that of the house of Atreus awaits him. On the level of the autobiography of the work, this signifies that a choice must be made between the story of Agamemnon's misfortunes and the story of Odysseus' victorious return. To choose the first is to continue in the tragic spirit of the *Iliad;* to choose the second, with Odysseus as the hero, is to propose the model of the return, which will liberate Ithaka from the new siege that holds it captive in the hands of the Suitors.

The nostalgia for the heroic epoch also prevails in Menelaos' house. In the king's words:

> So it is with no pleasure I am lord over all these possessions.
> You will have heard all this from your fathers, whoever
>   your fathers
> are, for I have suffered much, and destroyed a household
> that was very strongly settled and held many goods within it.
> I wish I lived in my house with only a third part of all
> these goods, and that the men were alive who died in those
>   days
> in wide Troy land far away from horse pasturing Argos.
> Still and again lamenting all these men and sorrowing
> many a time when I am sitting here in our palace
> I will indulge my heart in sorrow, and then another time
> give over, for surfeit of gloomy lamentation comes quickly.
>
> [IV, 93–103]

Helen puts a drug in the wine, which induces the pleasures of recounting and listening; and she herself recalls her meeting with Odysseus disguised as a beggar in the streets of Troy, when she recognized but did not betray him. This memory prefigures Odysseus' disguise on his return to Ithaka, where, again clothed in rags, he will move through the ranks of his enemies with the aim of destroying them. Next Menelaos recalls the incident of the wooden horse, as husband and wife vie with each other to furnish Telemachos with an image of his father that will conform to what he is seeking.

It is apparent from the stories heard by Telemachos that Homer too perceives that the hero he requires must be endowed with shrewdness and guile, for only such a one will be able to accomplish the attempted return, which is opposed to the clear and tragic truth of the model of the siege. Hence, the meaning of Telemachos' journey is that reality must be faced, assaulted, and finally dominated in such a way that there emerges from it the required story. This is the sense of the struggle between Menelaos and Proteus, which must serve as a lesson for Telemachos. Since thousands of individual destinies are concealed in reality, one must exert oneself to extract from it the story of Odysseus rather than that of Agamemnon. The world of the *Odyssey* is phantasmagoric and illusory, one where the boundaries between reality and delusion are fluctuating, like those between dreaming and waking. Yet reality exists and one must cope with it.

This is why in the *Odyssey* the human physiognomy is always on the verge of being distorted or of disappearing. When Odysseus emerges from the bushes before the astonished eyes of Nausikaa and her young companions, he appears a veritable beast.

> So speaking, great Odysseus came from under his thicket,
> and from the dense foliage with his heavy hand he broke off
> a leafy branch to cover his body and hide the male parts,
> and went in the confidence of his strength, like some
> hill-kept lion.
>
> [VI, 127–130]

But when he had bathed and clothed himself, he appeared "radiant in grace and good looks," which prompted Nausikaa to exclaim: "Now he even resembles one of the gods" (VI, 243). And Odysseus' answer broke forth: I am in no way like the Immortals, and do you know why? I have suffered enough to know I am not a god and to know I no longer want to be one; this is why I left Kalypso's island, refusing her offer of immortality; this is why I decided once more to confront all the human hazards of metamorphosis. Observe the signs of suffering in my face and hear them in my words; this will prove to you I am no god, but also that I am nothing less than a man.

Suffering is humanity's passport in this poem, which is nonetheless imbued with joy. In fact, when Odysseus arrives in the land of the Phaiakians, he again appears on the scene as a hero who must win his own identity. No one knows who he is, and he conceals his name; but when he finally discloses it in order to continue the bard's stories, once more the border between fact and fable is blurred. Odysseus assuredly knows more than does the bard about these stories, and he was also the sole witness to the deeds he recounts; no one can refute him. There is a common element to all of Odysseus' tales; throughout his tortuous journey he has done nothing but lose and find himself repeatedly, always improving his knowledge of the art of disguise, in which he was already an expert. To this end he was even willing to become Nobody, as in the episode of Polyphemos.

The hero wants to be again Odysseus, king of Ithaka and husband to Penelope; he wishes to become what he is, and this wish defines every effort to achieve identity. He knows he is fighting an all but impossible battle, impeded by fate and the gods. In a world in which the return is so difficult, Odysseus has to learn how to renounce even himself if necessary. The Cyclops episode is more or less at the beginning of Odysseus' adventures, as recounted by him at Alkinoös' court. Polyphemos, a relict of the old tyrannical, bloodthirsty gods, is not subject to the behests of Olympos, as he proudly proclaims to his prisoners in the cave; he is bound to daily work, to herding, milking, and creating implements which Odysseus finds in his cave. He is, in fact, the god of an age of shepherds, dedicated to the soil and animal husbandry—an age prior to the incursions of sea raiders, as personified by Odysseus. "Are you recklessly roving as pirates do?" inquires the suspicious Cyclops. To him, there is little difference between pirates and merchants; both are seafarers and, as such, not to be trusted. This encounter catches Odysseus momentarily off guard, and his appeal to Zeus, who is also the god of hospitality, incites Polyphemos to mockery. Confined in the cave, in the belly of the earth, Odysseus regresses significantly toward the womb of life as he finds himself caught in an elemental struggle for survival. Polyphemos signifies the return of wolf-men, of monsters like those who had obsessed the frontiers of consciousness in the earlier poem.

The episode of Polyphemos does not call for the usual similes of wild animals. We are now in a bestial world which is under the protection of a bestial divinity. The risk of the return is also the danger of being sucked back into the dark vertigo of primordial matter. Once again, chaos is the chief peril from which Homer's characters have to defend themselves. Odysseus' clever speech is shattered against Cyclops' carapace of indifference, as Polyphemos demonstrates a peculiar superiority—that of an animal if it was able to speak. Only after Odysseus has blinded him does Polyphemos suddenly realize that beasts, in fact, do not speak, that he is alone in a world now ruled by man. This is his lament in his speech to the ram:

> My dear old ram, why are you thus leaving the cave last of
> the sheep? Never in the old days were you left behind by
> the flock, but long-striding, far ahead of the rest would
>   pasture
> on the tender bloom of the grass, be first at running rivers,
> and be eager always to lead the way first back to the
>   sheepfold
> at evening. Now you are last of all. Perhaps you are grieving
> for your master's eye, which a bad man with his wicked
>   companions
> put out, after he had made my brain helpless with wine, this
> Nobody, who I think has not yet got clear of
>   destruction.
> *If only you could think like us and only be given*
> *a voice,* to tell me where he is skulking away from my anger.
>   [IX, 447–457; my italics]

In this passage Polyphemos mourns the loss of a purely

physical—that is, perfect—friendship, and at the same time laments the irrevocable decadence that sets in with the advent of the navigators, dwarfs, and ridiculous beggars—as he later characterizes them when venting his rage—the gravediggers of divine bestiality. The episode is made still more memorable by the fact that Odysseus is concealed beneath the ram, and it is thus to him that Cyclops unwittingly speaks. It is Odysseus who, clinging to the fleece of the animal's belly, succeeds in evading Cyclops' anxious hands as he vainly runs them over the ram's back; it is man who, in a momentary and unprecedented symbiosis, uses the animal for his own ends, and is able to outwit the Beast.

In order to escape from Polyphemos, Odysseus must suppress himself as a person. The trick he uses goes beyond a mere ruse. To call himself Nobody is to secure his physical survival by obliterating himself. But it also means to become Nobody, if only temporarily: in fact, to disappear in order finally to emerge from the dark womb of the cave. Now that the hero has embarked on the attempted return, he understands that his survival is linked to the ceaseless doubt of his own identity. Declaring himself Nobody is analogous to concealing himself in the ram's fleece. Faced with Cyclops' revelation—the divinity of man-beast—Odysseus chooses the course of total dissimulation, and in this unforeseen challenge he is forced to recognize the substance of reality. Polyphemos, who devours Odysseus' shipmates, is very remote from the serene figures of Olympos. Suddenly they are proved to be figures on a screen, a recondite film of fables, understatement pure and simple, their polite discourse entirely devoid of allusions to cannibalism or defecation. No god comes to Odysseus' aid in the cave; he is abandoned to his fate and must extricate himself and his crew without help. Nature is infernal, sanguinary, savage; and we are her sons and resemble her, since indeed she feeds on us: Polyphemos, "without leaving anything, ate them, entrails, flesh and the marrowy bones alike" (IX, 292–293).

Only he who bears the name Nobody can become Somebody; being Nobody, then, is the initial form of self-recognition. After

43

escaping by concealing himself under the ram, Odysseus can at last cry out to his defeated enemy:

> Cyclops, if any mortal man ever asks you who it was
> that inflicted upon your eye this shameful blinding,
> tell him that you were blinded by Odysseus, sacker of cities.
> Laertes is his father, and he makes his home in Ithaka.
>
> [IX, 502–505]

His companions cannot comprehend Odysseus' need to say all this to the giant; they implore him to set sail, and rightly, for the great stones hurled down by Polyphemos imperil their embarcation. We understand why it is so important for this hero to have recovered his pride of name, feeling as he does now that he has won it. Now Odysseus is worthy of his name; now he knows that he is Somebody.

The reader of the *Odyssey* is sure to be struck by the fact that there are no legendary monsters in the poem either before or after Odysseus' recital at Alkinoös' court. When Homer reverts to the third-person narrative, men and gods again share the stage, and monsters are no longer in evidence. Are we to conclude that Odysseus is the only falsifier, at least the only "fabricator" of intricate tales? Let us rather say the Odysseus has his own way of telling the truth about what actually happened to him, while at the same time concealing it in a series of events which retain the flavor and color of great nautical adventures. To understand what Odysseus is really saying, we must pursue the question of the meaning of the return.

The siege was a temporal as well as spatial model. Its temporal direction represents the irreversible movement of human history. The impossibility of the return was also based on the impossibility of a regression in time. When Odysseus begins his journey, he challenges this impossibility; and his story is a description of the various stages of a temporal regression toward the origins of humanity, to the borderland between man and

44

beast. Sometimes this border is crossed, as in the Circe episode when Odysseus' companions are turned into swine; more often the hero keeps himself in a state of precarious balance, trying not to be reabsorbed into the prehuman world. His victory is won when he learns to use the beast for his own ends, as in the case of the ram. The importance of the episode with Polyphemos, which occurs near the beginning of Odysseus' adventures, is clear. Now he knows the risks of his attempt to return; now, like a modern science-fiction hero, he knows that he is traveling in time as well as in space. And the sea is inhabited by enormous presences, buried in the memory of the human race and rediscovered by Odysseus.

When he is again in possession of his name, Odysseus reveals a richer and more adaptable personality. In the *Iliad* he appeared to be crafty and cold, the confederate of priests and politician of the siege. From now on, he assumes the burden of consciousness borne by Achilleus and Hektor in the earlier poem. The "reasonable" Odysseus of the siege undergoes a crisis at the outset of the return; traversing the Mediterranean is essentially a voyage of rediscovery of the self. If finding oneself means first knowing how to lose oneself (as demonstrated in the Polyphemos episode), then recognizing one's identity means running the risk of forgetting oneself.

Odysseus' entire journey is experienced as an obsession with the terror of oblivion. Even before Cyclops, there was the adventure in the land of the Lotus-Eaters. Two men had been sent ahead to reconnoiter the country.

> My men went on and presently met the Lotus-Eaters,
> nor did these Lotus-Eaters have any thoughts of destroying
> our companions, but they only gave them lotus to taste of.
> But any of them who ate the honey-sweet fruit of lotus
> was unwilling to take any message back, or to go
> away, but they wanted to stay there with the lotus-eating
> people, feeding on lotus, and forget the way home.
>   I myself

45

took these men back weeping, by force, to where the ships
    were,
and put them aboard under the rowing benches and tied
    them
fast.

[IX, 91–100]

In the climate of the *Iliad,* such an adventure would be incon-
ceivable. Yet to turn back means above all to risk forgetting, that
is, to revert to a preconscious level. This is why memory becomes
so important in the *Odyssey:* even the narrative structure, so
often articulated in recollection, sporadically demonstrates this
need. The Odysseus who remembers is he who fears he has
forgotten; there is a continual battle against the threat of a be-
clouded mind. The model of the return is built on the past,
whereas that of the siege is founded on the present, the time
prison that closes every breach.

When, at the outset of the voyage, someone tries to forestall
Odysseus, two of his companions, instead, fall victims to the
violence; the incident will be repeated, however, for the real
target is Odysseus' consciousness. At every stage of the voyage
the choice arises: speak or subside into oblivion. When men do
not inquire of Odysseus who he is, they are implicitly offering
him the lotus flower. In speaking of himself, Odysseus recovers
and reaffirms himself, and in the end escapes the amnesia of the
self; it almost seems that he is roving from shore to shore in
search of someone who is willing to listen to him. On the floating
island of Aiolos, whiling away his time in banquets and long,
soothing slumbers, Odysseus spends a month with his host.

and a whole month he entertained me and asked me
    everything
of Ilion, and the ships of the Argives, and the Achaians'
homecoming, and I told him all the tale as it happened.

[X, 14–16]

Odysseus is his own book, passing through thousands of hands on loan, eager to be opened. The Lotus-Eaters, who ask him no questions, leave the book sealed; he then must set out in search of one who will interrogate him, so that he can resume his narration: "and I told him all the tale as it happened" (x, 16).

At the end of his long sojourn, Aiolos presents him with a sack, warning him that it is not to be opened. Odysseus is wise enough to respect this injunction, but his shipmates cannot resist the temptation to open it, whereupon they discover that it contains the winds, which, when released, buffet them from coast to coast till they are swept back to the island of Aiolos. This time, however, he is enraged and drives them away. The next stage of their journey is the country of the Laistrygones, bestial giants who proceed to destroy all but one of the ships, along with their reckless navigators. Not surprisingly, these giants ask no questions. Nor, later, does Circe, as long as she succeeds in her aim of shackling the swine-men to the land. But when she offers Odysseus the drug of oblivion, the hero, forewarned by Hermes, threatens her with his sword, and only then does the enchantress exclaim:

What man are you and whence? Where are your city and
  your parents?

.   .   .   .   .

You are then resourceful Odysseus.

[x, 325, 330]

The alternatives are always the same: to be recognized or to sink into the night of the soul. The terror of darkness looms over this grand sunlit poem. The nightmare also arises in the kingdom of the Kimmerians, the country of eternal night where, in his continuous effort to keep memory alive, Odysseus puts to shore.

47

Of equal significance is the descent to Hades. There the soul of Teiresias inquires of Odysseus:

> Son of Laertes and seed of Zeus, resourceful Odysseus,
> how is it then, unhappy man, you have left the sunlight
> and come here, to look on dead men, and this place without
>   pleasure?
>
> [XI, 92–94]

The answer might have been: I seek to know whether I want to remember, asking memory itself.

Another revealing aspect of the visit to Hades concerns Elpenor, a young warrior who arrived there the previous day, having died in a fall from a roof while drunk. Odysseus and his companions have been instructed to go to Hades, but Elpenor has come by the direct route of death, and is there waiting for them when they arrive. He is already a memory to his friends, yet fears that he will die again if he is forgotten.

> ... my lord, I ask that you remember me,
> and do not go and leave me behind, unwept, unburied.
>
> [XI, 71–72]

This is the refrain of all the shades of warriors who throng around Odysseus.

The visit to Hades is made by an Odysseus who descends into his own memory with open eyes, while the Odysseus who roves the seas encountering monsters is the hero in the grip of a collective, archetypal past, for which the *Odyssey* is the first anthropological novel, the classical equivalent of what Dante's *Divine Comedy* will be for Christian civilization. The passage describing the meeting with the shade of Achilleus is symbolic of the passing of the torch. In different circumstances, it is now Odysseus who is the protagonist of consciousness.

Each of the souls in Hades foretells something for Odysseus; thus, it is possible to trace in memory the roots of one's destiny. It is also possible to discern clues, as when the soul of Agamemnon says to him:

> When you bring your ship in to your own dear country, do it
> secretly, not in the open.

[XI, 455-456]

The advice is a fundamental indication of the strategy of the return: if there is a hidden truth behind this voyage, it cannot be arrived at except through dissimulation and deceit. While the clear truth of the siege asks only to be revealed, the return is presented from the first as a colossal deception, like every attempt to give a positive meaning to human life. And if the return conceals an ultimate truth or ultimate deception, it will be proved only by the outcome. We are once again very far from the univocal spirit of the *Iliad*. So the idea of "adventure" is born of the challenge to reality, and composed of deceit as well as of violence: every moment of Odysseus' voyage is a struggle with Proteus.

At the court of Alkinoös, when Odysseus takes the place of the bard and speaks of himself, it is again for the purpose of being recognized. At that moment an event of paramount importance for the future of the narrative art occurs: the character who recounts his own story enters upon the scene. Nothing like this had been seen in the *Iliad;* but we know that it has become a matter of life and death for Odysseus to tell his own story: if he does not speak he is lost. Alkinoös' kingdom is the last stage of his journey before reaching Ithaka, and by then Odysseus is in a position to recapitulate the peregrinations that have led him through individual and collective memory. In the course of this evocation something occurs that alters the very structure of the narrative. He recalls that Circe directed him to go down among the dead, explaining to him exactly how to conduct himself, just as she had previously done in putting him on guard against the Sirens and the perils of Skylla and Charybdis. Still earlier,

Hermes had taught him how to protect himself against the spells of the sorceress; and in Hades the soul of Teiresias had prophesied the return and the drastic degradation of Ithaka. These revelations anticipate what is about to happen. In certain instances, as in the episode of the Sirens, Odysseus seems to be playing a time-honored role with the diligence of one who cannot permit himself to err. When he is involved in the exploit, it is almost like the verification of an hypothesis.

This type of situation is to be found throughout the *Odyssey*, but with far less frequency and intensity than in Odysseus' personal recollections. The province of the author-narrator is the past, carved out of the memory of the human race; if a character is introduced into this zone of light and provided in turn with memory, he performs as if he were placed between two mirrors, endlessly reflecting himself. Odysseus in present time conjures up the past in terms of the future. The characters who say to him, *Do this, don't do that,* are personifications of the logic of events which, when seen in retrospect, seem to him inevitable. In his own way Odysseus has discovered that the best way to recall an event is to render it foreseeable. The admonitions of Circe and Hermes are also an invitation to face reality in order to be better able to remember it: Go forth to meet memory, but do not let yourself be captured by it. The Sirens who entreat Odysseus with the promise of singing to him of the heroic exploits of the siege of Troy resort to the most insidious method of persuasion, that of imprisoning him in memory itself and never letting him go. To escape from such perils means to continue the journey, and therefore the escape constitutes the story of the journey; but when Odysseus ceases his narration, it means that the voyage has been impeded.

This is what happens after the episode of the cattle of Helios. His companions have feasted on the flesh of the animals and have perished as a consequence of the god's vengeance. Odysseus survives and escapes to Kalypso's island, where his memory founders. There years pass uneventfully, with nothing to recount; but when the time comes that Telemachos needs him,

Odysseus resumes the return. The period spent on Kalypso's island represents the moment of genuine defeat. It does not merit recounting. All those years are dismissed in a rancorous statement: I was a prisoner there; nothing more to be said. In escaping from Kalypso, Odysseus has understood, as did the soul of Achilleus, that the mirage of immortality conceals a trap; the immutable smile holds no further attraction for him. This Mediterranean haven can no more detain him than could the horrendous cave of Polyphemos. In his archetypal journey there is also an experience of self-deification; to escape from the island in the raft that he himself has built is to repossess a human dimension, the one that pertains to him.

By the time Odysseus lands on the island of the Phaiakians, he has completed his pilgrimage of memory. He is now mature, as is demonstrated by the episode with Nausikaa. In rejecting the young girl's love, he proves that he is capable of resisting the temptation to exchange his maturity for an illusory youthfulness. Nausikaa's admiration is clearly for the deeds of a charismatic hero, as will be that of Desdemona, centuries later, in Shakespeare's tragedy. Odysseus avoids Othello's mistake, which is to regard himself as the figure reflected in the eyes of innocent adoration. To be reborn to a new life cannot mean to pause and garner this tribute, thereby deflecting the course of his return.

Only the hero who has chosen to continue his journey can sleep the sleep of Odysseus on the ship that carries him back to Ithaka.

> ... a sleep gentle,
> the sweetest kind of sleep with no awakening, most like
> death.
>
> [XIII, 79–81]

This is the sleep that takes possession of

> ... a man with a mind like the gods for counsel, one whose
> spirit up to this time had endured much, suffering many

> pains; the wars of men, hard crossing of the big waters;
> but now he slept still, oblivious of all he
>   had suffered.
>
> [XIII, 89-92]

This salutary sleep indicates that Odysseus has cast off the oppressive weight of his long journey through memory; rest descends upon him in the form of temporary oblivion, after which he will be able to choose the memories that will serve his conquest.

In fact, the struggle is resumed on the beach of Ithaka. Odysseus wanders about without recognizing his fatherland, for Athene has spread a mist between his eyes and the landscape. The hero contends anew with his memory. Then the goddess appears, so that a complex interior itinerary is objectified and made communicable.

> ... Athene came near him
> likening herself in form to a young man, a herdsman
> of sheep, a delicate boy, such as the children of kings are.
>
> [XIII, 221-223]

To his anxious inquiry the goddess responds: We are in Ithaka; did you not know? A country of rocks and sheep, whose fame has even reached Troy.

Odysseus rejoices, but his joy is arid and incomplete. To know is still not to recognize. Then, as if by chance, he begins to tell his story—all lies, Homer warns even before Odysseus begins:

> but he did not tell her the truth, but checked that word from
>   the outset,
> forever using to every advantage the mind that was in him.
>
> [XIII, 254-255]

It is a tale of murder and vengeance and, in the end, of abandonment, creating the curious impression that Odysseus is retelling in reverse what has happened to him. According to his story, Phoenician men had forsaken him on the shore, after despoiling him of his riches, whereas we know that gifts had been bestowed upon him by the Phaiakians of Alkinoös' kingdom and he had been magnanimously transported to Ithaka. In one point only is he faithful to the facts—that he had slept during the voyage: "Weary as I was, the sweetness of sleep came upon me" (XIII, 282). At the conclusion of the tale, Athene smiles and resumes the shape of a woman.

> You wretch, so devious, never weary of tricks, then you
>   would not
> even in your own country give over your ways of deceiving
> and your thievish tales. They are near to you in your very
>   nature.
>   [XIII, 293–295]

Then, in a gesture of humility, Odysseus entreats the goddess to help him. Athene dispels the mist, the land *becomes visible*, and a new and deeper joy fills Odysseus' heart, a joy suffused with tears that impels him to kiss the ground. Through the telling of his story the hero has *won the right to recognize Ithaka*. In the *Odyssey*, to know how to tell a story (to know how to deceive) is one of the supreme virtues.

> Surely I was on the point of perishing by an evil
> fate in my palace, like Atreus' son Agamemnon, unless
> you had told me, goddess, the very truth of all that has
>   happened.
>   [XIII, 383–385]

But Athene would have told him nothing had he not passed the test of telling the story; art is a weapon against life, as Achilleus' shield has clearly taught us. Odysseus' shield is the word, the deceptive word that is a distorting mirror of the world.

The concluding section of the *Odyssey* dramatically propounds the contest between two models for the representation of reality. Athene has transformed Odysseus into a ragged, wrinkled old man, complete with staff and knapsack. It is the same figure that Helen had evoked for Telemachos: Odysseus inside the walls of Troy, like a germ of dissolution within the structure of the siege. Disguised anew, Odysseus makes his way first to the house of the "noble swineherd" Eumaios.

> He found him sitting in front, on the porch, where the lofty
> enclosure had been built, in a place with a view on all sides,
> both large and handsome, cleared all about, and it was the
>   swineherd
> himself who had built it, to hold the pigs of his absent
>   master,
> far from his mistress and from aged Laertes. He made it
> with stones from the field, and topped it off with shrubbery.
>   Outside
> he had driven posts in full circle, to close it on all sides.
>
> [XIV, 5–11]

Returned to his homeland as if by means of a magic spell, Odysseus contemplates the ineradicable truth of the siege after his prolonged peregrinations. At the portals of the kingdom to be reconquered stands Eumaios' house, a kind of microcosm as well as porter's lodge. With stunning precision, Homer identifies the image of the wall that encircles the swineherd and his animals—a foreshadowing of the configuration of Odysseus' palace, at the sight of which the disguised hero will later utter the revealing words:

> Eumaios, surely this is the handsome house of Odysseus.
> Easily it is singled out and seen among many,
> for one part is joined on to another, and the courtyard is

worked on
with wall and copings, and the doors have been well made,
        with double
panels. Nobody could belittle this house.

[XVII, 264–268]

Having ranged the world, in the end Odysseus discovers the
model he had been challenging throughout his entire voyage:
walls that enclose a promise of happiness. In the lands where he
had been held prisoner, confronting the monsters that had
threatened to devour or enchain him—at every stage of the
journey there had been the possibility of falling back into a
closed world from which there is no escape. Moreover, the sea is
a mirage of freedom; on Achilleus' shield Homer had depicted
the ocean girding the land, the water confining the land as walls
enclose a besieged city. Even the theater of action of the return,
the land-enclosed Mediterranean sea, is a dungeon of the universal prison; and Odysseus is a fugitive fleeing along an aqueous corridor, skirting the cells that open to incarcerate him
again.

Now, before Odysseus' eyes, the Suitors are laying siege to
Penelope and rapaciously consuming his goods, all the while
pursued by the specters evoked by Phemios. Odysseus will transform this carousal-siege, if only momentarily, into epic theater.
The first to understand the meaning of the return, he now must
recognize anew the verity of the siege.

In the earlier poem Odysseus had been the most convinced
advocate of the logic of the siege and had tried to live pragmati-
cally, without questioning himself deeply—as if to say, Life being
what it is, one may as well make the best of it. His transformation is indicative of some of the most profound reflections on
man in Western literature. The revolts of Achilleus and Hektor
could not have jeopardized the siege, for it is the very structure
of reality, though they unquestionably hastened the end by dis-
seminating wrath and anguish. The level of consciousness re-

flected eventually becomes unendurable; and the model of the return presents itself as an ingenious remedy. Odysseus, the hero destined for a new incarnation, is chosen expressly because of his pragmatic qualities, his talent for adapting himself to unforeseen situations, his refusal to accept tragedy, and his ability to utilize every device, including the word. It is he who, with the artifice of the Trojan horse, symbolically destroyed the model of the siege—which means that a new stage of consciousness had to be found to ensure mankind's survival. One must defy time and turn back to memory, both of the individual and of the species.

Yet Odysseus would be no better than a vulgar liar, a common adventurer, were he not capable of perceiving reality. He knows that the siege continues to be the reality of man's situation in the world; indeed, he finds a state of siege wherever he goes, and in every instance endeavors to escape from it (the legend of his final voyages only confirms this attitude). The Greek myths often represent the great voyages as quests for something that has been lost, as in the case of the Argonauts and their search for the Golden Fleece. In this sense every journey, properly speaking, is a return: every journey is the spatialization of an event that is essentially temporal and hence inherent in consciousness. To circumvent the situation of stalemate, which the miserable consciousness of Achilleus and Hektor has rendered almost insupportable, Odysseus proposes an adventure that is also a challenge: Let us delve into this space-time that encompasses us, and who knows but that we may find something. And if we are obliged to practice deception, then so be it; anything that conduces to the prolongation of life is a positive factor.

It is worth noting that in the colloquy in Hades, the shade of Achilleus also expresses himself in these new "Odyssean" terms which permeate the spirit of the *Odyssey*. Life alone is of value, declares Achilleus. I would willingly be a slave if I could but live again.

At Alkinoös' court, Odysseus was able to convince his listeners by means of that human weapon par excellence, the *word;* and he will be obliged to do the same at Ithaka—this time to comply with the advice of Agamemnon and Athene to conceal his identity. Again Odysseus is Nobody. His aim is recognition, the supreme test of himself: *Let us see whether you are worthy of being Odysseus.* Clad in the traditional rags of misery, he assumes nonexistence once more. If man had retained his infallible animal instinct, everyone would have recognized him, as does Argos, his dog, which is described in a passage comparable to Cyclops' monologue for its poetry of animality. The animal kingdom, the world in which one is recognized by the sense of smell, is extinct—as is implied by the death of Argos soon after he recognizes his master. Wherever man appears with the word, the integrity of instinct is lost forever. In his anthropological exploration, Odysseus discovers that memory, the territory he courageously undertook to explore, is not unknown to his dog. And he also learns that human memory requires a stupendous effort to compensate for the loss of that simple yet formidable weapon, instinct.

In fact, none of the human beings recognizes Odysseus at first sight, not Eumaios, or Telemachos, or Penelope—the last not even when he has unmasked himself and strung the bow. Eurykleia alone detects a resemblance to the Odysseus she remembers, but only when she sees the scar on his thigh is his identity revealed to her. As his old nurse, she is the last remaining link between the instinctual and the conscious life. There is still a vestige of the mother animal in her, although she is too much a human being to have retained the unerring instinct of Argos; for her a sign, the scar, is needed, and on seeing it she voices her regret: I was unable to recognize you *at once.* The others fail to discover in the newcomer any resemblance to Odysseus, just as he at first failed to recognize Ithaka and had to lie to Athene in order to acquire that recognition; and now, in his slow approach to the still hidden center, he will have to lie to everyone he encounters. If he relinquishes his disguise he is lost—a consequence which is the meaning of the adventure of the return.

From the time man accepts the challenge of giving a positive meaning to life, he can no longer permit himself to give up lying.

Eumaios and Penelope, each in his or her own way, seem almost eager to help him concoct his fictions. Eumaios says:

> Come, old sir, along to my shelter, so that you also
> first may be filled to contentment with food and wine, then
> tell me
> where you come from, and about the sorrows you have been
> suffering.
>
> [XIV, 45–47]

And later, Penelope inquires of him:

> Stranger, I myself first have a question to ask you.
> What man are you and whence? Where is your city? Your
> parents?'
>
> [XIX, 104–105]

The hero could not wish for a more propitious inducement; to both he relates his invented tales, employing the same procedure he had used with Athene, mingling the true with the false. A very subtle relationship is established between Odysseus and Eumaios. Abandoning the legendary exploits he had conjured up at the court of Alkinoös, the hero descends to a more romanesque sphere, one replete with unexpected events of a purely external nature, thus anticipating the late classic novel and the medieval Mediterranean stories that converge in Boccaccio. But, quite appositely, Eumaios too has a story to relate.

> My guest, since indeed you are asking me all these
> questions,
> listen in silence and take your pleasure, and sit there
> drinking

your wine. These nights are endless, and a man can sleep
    through them,
or he can enjoy listening to stories, and you have no need
to go to bed before it is time.

[xv, 390–394]

And Eumaios tells a story which, though probably true, is no
less extraordinary and romantic than the one recounted by
Odysseus. This exchange between Eumaios and his master-guest
is replete with irony. After Odysseus has made a prodigious
effort of imagination, the servant tells him a true story that vies
with his in improbability. This represents another step in the
autobiography of the work in explicit *ars poetica* terms. Of two
stories, it is not the truer but rather the more probable one that
is convincing. The tales of the encounters with Circe and the
Sirens are far more credible than those of pirates, because they
are charged with symbolic and archetypal meaning, which is all
that makes a story credible. The principles of rhetoric (*inventio,
dispositio, narratio*) are ineffectual when this animating property
is wanting in a story.

Therefore in Homer we see not only the first example of the
romanesque spirit but also the first critique and ironic dissolution
of this spirit. The difference between the Odysseus who relates
his stories at Alkinoös' court and the Odysseus who regales
Eumaios with diverting tales is that between the narrator who
makes every element obligatory and inevitable and the storyteller who is incapable of finding the implicit order within an ac-
cumulation of events. The latter's stories resemble the events of
life as recounted by Eumaios: all the episodes are interchange-
able, given the immense richness of life itself. Art can never
compete with the manifold of reality; one of the secrets of art is
condensation.

Odysseus' stories all form part of his disguise; still others, in
the course of his endeavors, have been either used as aids or
discarded as too hazardous. Odysseus does not want Penelope to

59

know who he is till the final moment, and even Eumaios is kept in the dark; because they both despair of his return, they are to be rewarded for their fidelity but not regarded as peers. Telemachos, on the other hand, who awaits him with confidence, is immediately made privy to the secret. Odysseus must reach the center of himself and therefore must distinguish between friends and enemies without entertaining illusions about either. In the guise of a beggar, he claims his seigneurial rights; and at the end he spares only Phemios, who has found the expedient words for beseeching grace as though from an equal.

> I am at your knees, Odysseus. Respect me, have mercy.
> You will be sorry in time to come if you kill the singer
> of songs, I sing to the gods and to human people, and I am
> taught by myself, but the god has inspired in me the
>   song-ways
> of every kind, I am such a one as can sing before you
> as to a god. Then do not be furious to behead me.
>
> [xxii, 344–349]

Odysseus himself could have said the same; and it is this that makes his relations with the bard so suggestive. Phemios has kept watch over the action from the start; the everyday mediocrity has been lulled by his songs in celebration of the heroes. He has brought tears to the eyes of Penelope and the Suitors, prompted Telemachos to leave Ithaka in search of safety, and even now, when Odysseus has returned, fills the air with his songs. If the world evoked by Phemios represents the overwhelming presence of the great model, the appearance of Odysseus (this Telemachos now matured and ready for victory) permits open competition between the old and new models of reality. This rivalry signifies the recovery of the epic force and affirms the possibility of the return.

Thus Odysseus, while contending against the Suitors and preparing their destruction, also vies with the bard, and in a way less mysterious than might appear, since we know that the Homeric characters, from Achilleus to Odysseus, reflect the problems of their creator and are, in a sense, his spokesmen. The imbalance of tension between the world evoked by the great model and the real world generates the action of the *Odyssey:* the departure of Telemachos, the return of Odysseus. Odysseus' aims are both to transmute words into deeds and to take Phemios' place. Oddly, it is the swineherd Eumaios who introduces the metaphorical mission of the bard when, responding to the arrogance of Antinoös, leader of the Suitors, he asserts:

> Antinoös, though you are noble, this was not well spoken.
> For who goes visiting elsewhere so as to call another
> stranger, unless he is one who works for the people, either
> a prophet, or a healer of sickness, or a skilled workman,
> or inspired singer, one who can give delight by his singing?
> These are the men who all over the endless earth are
> invited.
>
> [XVII, 381–386]

Where the activity of the poet is compared to that of a skilled workman and of a prophet, the first analogy will quickly be exploited by Homer. The second will later find a distinct echo in a Dantean episode. Throughout the Middle Ages the poet will often be compared to a prophet, and Virgil, Dante's guide, will acquire fame as both poet and prophet or soothsayer.

Certainly the momentous concept of the return, linked to the voyage and the need to find roots, had to be born in the soul of a bard, an uprooted fugitive, who ends by finding many resemblances between his own destiny and that of Odysseus. Between the two "masters of their own domain" a rapport, a solidarity of an almost professional nature is established. Odysseus spares Phemios in the course of the slaughter and even smiles upon him benevolently; he is aware that he owes him much, perhaps his very existence. If Phemios had not sung of heroes, and consequently of him, Odysseus would not have returned, because no one would have expected him; at once bard and hero, Odys-

seus is the rival and the perpetuator of Phemios. Speaking of
Odysseus to Penelope, Eumaios says:

> but he has not yet told the story of all his suffering.
> But as when a man looks to a singer, who has been given
> from the gods the skill with which he sings for delight of
>   mortals,
> and they are impassioned and strain to hear it when he sings
>   to them,
> so he enchanted me in the halls as he sat beside me.
>
> [XVII, 517–521]

Yet the definitive image is that of Odysseus intent upon handling his own bow, which no one has succeeded in stringing.

> As when a man, who well understands the lyre and singing,
> easily, holding it on either side, pulls the strongly twisted
> cord of sheep's gut, so as to slip it over a new peg,
> so, without any strain, Odysseus strung the great bow.
> Then plucking it in his right hand he tested the bowstring,
> and it gave him back an excellent sound like the voice of a
>   swallow.
>
> [XXI, 406–411]

Odysseus the hero and Odysseus the narrator are united in the
image; now we know without doubt that the voyage is at the
same time the story of the voyage. The hero writes his story with
his arrows; and the bard might well have wished that his songs
had also been darts.

But even after all the proofs, even after the slaughter of the
Suitors, Penelope fails to recognize Odysseus—which clearly indicates that he has not yet attained the heart of his own identity
or anything analogous to the center of Achilleus' shield. After
having circled the globe, just where in his home is he to find that
which is most dear to him, that which more than anything else
should be remembered? It is the "circumspect Penelope" who

subjects him to the final test by letting him understand that the nuptial bed has been removed. The hero's ire is aroused, and he embarks on a long and exhaustive description of the bed, thereby confirming his true identity. By the end of his discourse, Penelope has no further doubt, and the recognition has been effected.

There is abundant evidence that this last episode is to be read in a symbolic light. Consider the construction of the bed.

> There was the bole of an olive tree with long leaves growing
> strongly in the courtyard, and it was thick, like a column.
> I laid down my chamber around this, and built it, until I
> finished it, with close-set stones, and roofed it well over,
> and added the compacted doors, fitting closely together.
> Then I cut away the foliage of the long-leaved olive
> and trimmed the trunk from the roots up, planing it with a
>   brazen
> adze, well and expertly, and trued it straight to a chalkline,
> making a bed post of it, and bored all holes with an auger.
> I began with this and built my bed, until it was finished,
> and decorated it with gold and silver and ivory.
> Then I lashed it with thongs of oxhide, dyed bright with
>   purple.
>
> [XXIII, 190–201]

This tree is at the center of a new, immutable image of siege; but it becomes house and bed, without losing contact with its own roots. (Odysseus had not uprooted it.) Was this not what the hero had been obscurely seeking far and wide on his voyages? Was this not what made his return worthwhile? "There is one particular feature in the bed's construction. I myself, no other man, made it" (XXIII, 188–189). It is therefore something which, although shared with Penelope, is fundamentally his own.

Certainly Odysseus has never before expressed so profound a feeling about his own creativity; even after the great massacre of the Suitors, his words seemed to minimize the personal import of the event: "These were destroyed by the doom of the gods and their own hard actions" (XXII, 413). Now, however, he is evoking something less heroic, but something he has constructed without the aid of any other man. Somewhat earlier the work of the poet was compared to that of a skilled workman; the artisan Odysseus, who has already built his own ship, finds his own deepest level in this memory of himself as creator. It is the point at which the autobiography of the work is definitely welded to the model of the return; the vision of the siege is no longer contested but accepted, since the tree-bed reaffirms man's entire effort to shape his own destiny. It requires the long, far-flung voyage into his past and that of the human race to arrive at this simple yet profound conclusion. Penelope then is not the object of the return, but only the consolation prize. On the tree-bed Odysseus finds himself completely. For a narrator—and perhaps also for a hero—to find himself is to remember, to know how to live in the world. The great storyteller resides in a corner of himself which no one can invade, close to the ineradicable trunk. Art, like love, draws its life from a plant that has been shaped by one's own hands.

We understand why, after an experience like that of the *Iliad,* the *Odyssey* was necessary. The great value of the tragic vision of life is that of hitting the target of truth: life is tragic; the statement requires no special emphasis. When one has arrived at such a conclusion, and with the artistic force and trenchancy of the *Iliad,* there remains little to be added. The *Odyssey* depicts the endeavor to start a new life, even at the cost of deception. The hero of such a struggle can be no one but Odysseus. If, to survive, Odysseus has to resort to disguise, art must do likewise; if the hero is prepared to deceive, so must be the bard who sings of him. Aristotle was undoubtedly thinking more of the *Odyssey* than of the *Iliad* when he wrote in his *Poetics:* "Homer more than any other has taught the rest of us the art of framing lies in the right way."

And the lie became conscious, as is proved by the presence of Demodokos and Phemios. When art becomes conscious of its own *modus operandi,* it ends by projecting the shadow of the author upon the scene of the work—as will be seen in Dante, in his treatment of all the poets who inhabit the hereafter, and again in Shakespeare, in his presentation of the professional actors who intervene in *Hamlet.* It is not surprising that the *Odyssey* has always been regarded as more "modern" than the *Iliad.* Posterity has felt in it a will to endure, to survive, that contrasts with the spirit of the *Iliad,* which not by chance ends with a funeral.

For centuries the two models, the siege and the return, have confronted each other and have sometimes intermingled. Neither succeeds in definitively prevailing, and this is one of the reasons for the continual renewal of Western literature. The return can avoid the tragic confirmation only at the cost of endless expedients, among them the device of the happy ending. When the truth of the siege is represented, nothing remains but to begin another voyage. According to the post-Homeric legends, Odysseus set out anew. One of these legends came down to Dante.

3

The Meeting with Geryon

What is the meaning of "comedy" in Dante? There seems to be no satisfactory answer to this question. In a letter written in Latin to Can Grande della Scala, the Veronese prince who was his friend and patron, Dante explains the meaning of the poem's title in terms both of its form and content. The poem, he states, describes an action that begins tragically but ends happily, rather than the reverse; moreover, it is written in the vernacular instead of Latin, the noble, scholarly language required for tragedy, and should therefore be termed a comedy. This explanation seems so awkward, so inconsistent with Dante's genius, that a number of critics have cast serious doubt upon the authenticity of the letter. The problem is that from a philological point of view the letter appears to be unquestionably genuine. The most cogent comment on the issue is the observation by Curtius: "Dante's title was a makeshift."

Yet there remains another possibility, one which I propose to explore in this essay. What if Dante, as the acknowledged author of the *Letter to Can Grande,* had expressed something other than what he actually believed concerning the title of the poem? And if he did, what was the motivation for such an attempt at disguise?

The *Letter to Can Grande,* in which Dante states that he is working on the *Paradiso,* was written after the completion of the

66

Inferno and the *Purgatorio*. The word "comedy" appears only twice in the poem, both times in the *Inferno:* first in Canto XVI, line 128, and then in Canto XXI, line 2. And nowhere else does it appear. Let us see if it is possible to find a solution to the doubts by analyzing the meaning of the word in the context of the episodes in which it is used.

The first episode is dominated by the terrifying presence of Geryon. Among the extrinsic indications of the importance of his appearance is the fact that the end of the episode marks the halfway point in the *Inferno*—a coincidence that is certainly not without design in Dante's structural strategy. The roar of the river Phlegethon falling from the seventh to the eighth circle opens the scene with a deafening prelude:

> che 'l suon del'acqua n'era sì vicino,
> che per parlar saremmo a pena uditi.
>
> [*Inferno,* XVI, 92–93]

. . . the sound of the water was so near that we could scarcely have heard each other speak.

The entire episode is dominated by the resounding water, though not until somewhat later, not until the descent on Geryon's back is there another reference to it:

> Io sentia già da la man destra il gorgo
> far sotto noi un orribile scroscio.
>
> [XVII, 118–119]

I heard now on our right the whirlpool making a horrible roaring below us.

Although the water is never described in visual images—only its sounds reach Dante—one knows that it is near without being seen. This presence provides an extraordinary setting for the scene, a sonorous backdrop looming behind an essentially abstract landscape, a margin of land on the brink of the abyss. The incessant howling of Phlegethon is unquestionably a cry of horror expressed through the medium of the setting: the horror of the void proclaimed by hell itself in the precipitous, suicidal cascade. Where will the river end? We shall never know. The ravine cleaves inferno in two, both structurally and topographically.

Something quite different will begin with Malebolge; even the first mention will give a sense of a sudden, isolated apparition, almost a new *incipit* after the dark wood of the first canto.

> Luogo è in inferno detto Malebolge.
>
> [XVIII, 1]

> There is a place in hell called Malebolge.

The sonorous water falling headlong and irrevocably into the abyss has its visual correspondent in the infernal air, which here is particularly viscid and malign. It is a "thick and murky air," treacherous and stagnant, the veritable breath of the abyss; one must bear in mind that Dante's cry of amazement at the end of Canto XVI is not caused by the figure of Geryon alone, glimpsed from afar yet in its entirety, but by the fact that the figure *swims in air,* like a kind of aerial fish, unnatural and sinister:

> . . . i' vidi per quell'aere grosso e scuro
>   venir notando una figura in suso,
>   maravigliosa ad ogne cor sicuro.
>
> [XVI, 130–132]

> I saw, through that thick and murky air, come swimming upwards a figure amazing to every steadfast heart.

"Swimming," not flying; and so that the reader shall be left in no doubt, Dante follows the passage with an aquatic simile:

si come torna colui che va giuso
    talora a solver l'ancora ch'aggrappa
o scoglio o altro che nel mare è chiuso.

[XVI, 133-135]

even as he returns who sometimes goes down to loose the
anchor that is caught on a reef or something else hidden in
the sea.

In the following canto Geryon is compared to boats that lie
partly in water and partly on land, to a beaver, then again to a
bark, and immediately afterward to an eel:

Come la navicella esce di loco
    in dietro in dietro, sì quindi si tolse;
    e poi ch'al tutto si sentì a gioco,
là 'v' era 'l petto, la coda rivolse,
    e quella tesa, come anguilla, mosse,
    e con le branche l'aere a se raccolse.

[XVII, 100-105]

As the bark backs out little by little from its place, so Geryon
withdrew thence; and when he felt himself quite free, he
turned his tail to where his breast had been, and, stretching
it out, moved it like an eel, and with his paws gathered the
air to himself.

And during the descent, "Ella sen va notando lenta lenta" (He
goes swimming slowly on. [XVII, 115]).

In the series of images which allude to the unheard-of nature
of Geryon (of particular significance is the fact that, in contrast
to the other mythological figures in the *Inferno,* Geryon is silent,
mute as a fish and emitting no sound of any sort), there are two

69

similes that refer to a realm totally different from the sea, that of flight. Mounted on Geryon's croup, Dante compares himself to two mythological personages, Phaëthon and Icarus:

> Maggior paura non credo che fosse
>   quando Fetonte abbandonò li freni,
>   per che 'l ciel, come pare ancor, si cosse;
> né quando Icaro misero le reni
>   sentí spennar per la scaldata cera,
>   gridando il padre a lui "Mala via tieni!"
>
> [XVII, 106–111]

I do not think that there was greater fear when Phaëthon let loose the reins, whereby the sky as yet appears, was scorched, nor when the wretched Icarus felt his loins unfeathering by the melting wax, and his father cried to him, "You go an ill way!"

At the final stage of their descent, Geryon suddenly seems to lose his fishlike nature and to resemble a bird, a falcon:

> Come 'l falcon che'è stato assai su l'ali,
>   che sanza veder logoro o uccello
>   fa dire al falconiere: "Ome, tu cali!"
> discende lasso onde si move isnello,
>   per cento rote, e da lunge si pone
>   dal suo maestro, disdegnoso e fello...
>
> [XVII, 127–132]

As the falcon that has been long on the wing—that, without seeing lure or bird, makes the falconer cry, "Ah, ah, you're coming down!"—descends weary, with many a wheeling, to where it set out swiftly, and alights disdainful and sullen, far from its master...

The comparison is the more disconcerting because this falcon descends without its prey, whereas Geryon bears two persons on his back. Is it possible that Dante was not aware of this difference? Whenever Dante appears to be abstracted, it is we who should be more alert.

Let us return to the beginning of the episode, to the passages following the thunder of the cataract. As a lure, to draw Geryon to them, Virgil throws into the abyss the cord Dante wears around his waist.

> Io avea una corda intorno cinta,
>   e con essa pensai alcuna volta
>   prender la lonza alla pelle dipinta.
> Poscia ch'io l'ebbi tutta da me sciolta,
>   sì come 'l duca m'avea comandato,
>   porsila a lui aggroppata e ravvolta.
> Ond'ei si volse inver'lo destro lato,
>   e alquanto di lunge dalla sponda
>   la gittò giuso in quell'alto burrato.
>
> [XVI, 106-114]

I had a cord girt round me, and with it I once thought to take the gay-skinned leopard. After I had quite loosed it from me, as my leader bade, I passed it to him knotted and coiled. Whereon he, turning to the right, flung it some distance out from the edge, down into the depth of that abyss.

What is this cord? Dante has made no prior allusion to it. One might think that it has suddenly appeared on his person, that the poet has only just invented it for the immediate requirement of the episode; but this is not so. Dante makes quite clear the fact that he has been wearing it from the very beginning of his journey, but only now is he able to acknowledge its existence. As was apparent to the earliest commentators, the cord represents fraud: it is the snare by means of which Dante thought it possible to capture the leopard (another image of fraud). Later we shall see what manner of fraud Dante has used in order to combat the beast. For the moment, let us simply observe that the situation seems to imply that the one way of dominating fraud is by resorting to another, more subtle form of deception, at least until divine justice has pronounced the judgment that puts an end to any possibility of intrigue.

An outstanding feature of the *Commedia* is that Dante permits only those truths which have fully ripened to be represented. He refers to the cord at this point because only now does it appear to him to be an indispensable instrument for the journey in progress. Therefore, these lines depict the passage from the stage at which Dante uses the cord semiconsciously to the stage at which it must be recognized openly before he descends into the pit of Malebolge. The first step is for Dante to recognize the existence of the cord encircling his own body, and the second is to hand it to Virgil—that is, to consign it to the light of reason. He passes it to him "knotted and coiled"—ostensibly to facilitate the its handling, but also to suggest the serpentine nature of the cord-fraud. Like a serpent, in fact, it wraps itself around another body, but once detached from that body it recoils of itself. Because Dante does not say that it was he who wound it, he suggests a mysterious life animating the cord.

The two poets now stand waiting on the brink of the abyss, Virgil peering into the chasm and Dante with his eyes fixed on him.

> "E' pur convien che novità risponda,"
>   dicea fra me medesmo, "al novo cenno
>   che 'l maestro con l'occhio sì seconda."
>
> [XVI, 115–117]

> "Surely," I said to myself, "something strange will answer the strange signal which the master so follows with his eye."

Dante's attention is focused on his master, as if expecting the revelation to arise from him; he trusts implicitly in his rational guide, who has just directed his attention to the depths of the chasm, the shadowy gloom of the unconscious. Dante has perhaps never expressed so completely as in this arduous contemplation of the abyss the symbolic character of the subterranean exploration of the soul which constitutes his passage through inferno. Indeed, the entire journey is a descent to the nether world, there to encounter the monsters that inhabit it in order to recognize and overcome them. He desires to confront the specters that haunt his bewildered days, the animals sent to hunt him down by the demons raging in those depths. Long before the professional investigators of the soul, the poets understood that descent must precede ascent. Virgil reads Dante's thoughts and announces to him that one of the monsters vaguely envisioned by his disciple will assume real body, form, and dimension, and will emerge from the unconscious to be "discovered" to the poet's sight:

El disse a me: "Tosto verrà di sovra
ciò ch'io attendo, e che il tuo pensier sogna:
tosto convien ch'al tuo viso si scovra."

[XVI, 120-123]

"Soon will come up what I look for and what your mind dreams of," he said to me; "soon must it be discovered to your sight."

The appearance of Geryon is, in fact, an *emersion,* indicated by the image of a mariner who rises to the surface after diving into the sea to release an entangled anchor, thereby eliminating a hindrance to the continuation of a voyage. The figure of Geryon inspires Dante not only with terror but also a sense of liberation, as if the poet now apprehends the necessity for this encounter to the unmooring of his ship of pilgrimage. Later, Geryon will be described as a "bark"; thus, beast though he is, he will be identified, at least momentarily, with Dante's ship, which he will be without ceasing to be Geryon. Dante will *use* Geryon; he will take full advantage of the overwhelming figure of Fraud.

In this exceedingly dense passage Dante is contending with two problems simultaneously; either would be enough to daunt the most intrepid pilgrim. For Geryon, according to my interpretation, represents Fraud both morally and aesthetically: he is the personification of the poetic lie. The significance of the cord that girds Dante from the outset of his journey becomes clear: the poet suddenly understands the necessity of coming to terms with the poetic disguise essential to his creative effort. Now we see Geryon depicted by Virgil as the beast "that infects the world," then by Dante as the "foul image of fraud." It is no longer possible to look the other way and pretend Geryon is not there. He *is* there, face to face with Dante.

> La faccia era faccia d'uom giusto,
>   tanto benigna avea di fuor la pelle,
>   e d'un serpente tutto l'altro fusto;
> due branche avea pilose insin l'ascelle;
>   lo dosso e 'l petto e ambedue le coste
>   dipinti avea di nodi e di rotelle.
> Con più color, sommesse e sovraposte
>   non fer mai drappi Tartari ne Turchi,
>   né fuor tai tele per Aragne imposte.
>
> [XVII, 10–18]

His face was the face of a just man, so benign was its outward aspect, and all his trunk was that of a serpent; he had two paws, hairy to the armpits; his back and breast and both his sides were painted with knots and circlets. Tartars or Turks never made cloth with more colors of groundwork and pattern, nor were such webs laid on the loom by Arachne.

The "knots and circlets," symbols of tricks, exert an aesthetic fascination on Dante, and this is confirmed by the comparisons

74

he resorts to: cloth made by Tartars and Turks and webs from the loom of Arachne—works of art in which the craft of weaving has reached its acme. But the moral problem is inseparable from the aesthetic one; Dante does not choose these terms of comparison without intent: Tartars and Turks (antichrists, or at any rate anti-Christians by definition) and Arachne, she who would challenge Minerva—all exemplars of the fierce pride of the artist who exceeds his limits and enters into a temerarious contest with God. Geryon's designs are even more complex and beguiling, which is hardly surprising, since Dante perceives in them more than a symbol of moral trickery: he sees the richness of poetic elaboration he needs for the pursuance of his journey, sees the necessity of using the lie in order to recount the journey—to *make* the journey.

We have come in fact to the crucial point of the confrontation with Geryon. He is presented with "the face of a just man" superimposed on the body of a beast embellished with the patterns of fraud. At the end of the previous canto, just before the apparition of the monster, Dante had addressed to the reader one of those frenetic outbursts typical of the anxious poet who fears that the reader may miss the deeper significance of the mise-en-scène:

> Sempre a quel ver c'ha faccia di menzogna
> de' l'uom chiuder le labbra fin ch'el puote,
> però che sanza colpa fa vergogna;
> ma qui tacer non posso.
>
> [XVI, 124–127]

To that truth which has the face of a lie a man should always close his lips so far as he can, for through no fault of his it brings reproach; but here I cannot be silent.

It is truly strange that the desired parallelism (and concomitant antithesis) between Geryon's "face of a just man" and the "face of a lie" ascribed to the "truth" should have passed unnoticed by the reader. This is not the first time that Dante has described an incredible apparition, but now he seems to be prompted by the need to reassure the reader in some way, to implore him to trust in the poet's good faith. The reassurance is a master stroke used in anticipation: the vision of Geryon could arouse in the reader the suspicion (already a certainty for Dante) that beneath the veracious surface of a story is concealed the fraud of a lie, and beneath the confident tone of an account of a journey is concealed a tissue of fables that would be the envy of the Turks and of Arachne. The defensive move consists in reversing this possible interpretation by the reader; Dante presents himself as one who is at grips with a truth so surprising that it appears to be a lie and, indeed, seems to excuse himself for his own implausibility:

> ... e per le note
> di questa comedìa, lettor, ti giuro
> s'elle non sien de lunga grazia vòte.
>
> [XVI, 127–129]

... and, reader, I swear to you by the notes of this Comedy—so may they not fail of lasting favor.

"Reader, I swear to you." When has Dante ever had to swear? Because the vehemence of his attempt at persuasion has become extreme, he now must find something to swear by, something dearer than all else, more precious than life itself—in short, the work that he perceives as life redeemed, a vibrant retaliation against fate. If I do not speak the truth, may my verses soon be forgotten. But if his verses are forgotten, of what importance will be the truth, much less the story? Hence Dante knows quite well that credibility must be won primarily on the poetic level: if he writes well, he will be believed. And however he confronts Geryon, Dante's problem is essentially the same: a truth that depends upon its way of being presented always contains a degree of deception—especially when one sets out to describe the indescribable, the supernatural world beyond sensory experience.

So now Dante confronts the full weight of the lie that he is to bear throughout his journey-narrative. Charon, the Minotaur, the Centaurs, and now Geryon; the tempest, rivers of blood, thickets of gnarled trees, and cascades of fire—all these express the striving to translate into human language and human fantasies the mystery of the Christian hereafter, the anguish that a certain modern aestheticism would wish to erase from the medieval mentality. The age of Saint Thomas, of the "logical proofs" of the existence of God, the age of the nominalists, the age of Dante would not have "spontaneously" believed in the supernatural. Essentially, the culture of the late Middle Ages existed in a nostalgic dimension of relation to the divine; it was an epoch replete with oneiric tremors and methodical pedantic inquiries in which the infancy of Christianity appears bathed in the same mythical light as the classic fables.

In the purgatorial visions Dante will evoke episodes of the Gospels together with the memorable deeds of Trajan, and he seems not to treat them differently. Hence the conception of Christ in his work as a powerful but remote figure; the God-man is less a reality to Dante than an idea. The intermediary between the poet and God is Beatrice, a figure more abstract and at the same time more personal than the God who descends to walk among men. An exceedingly artful and erudite poet, entirely lacking in naïveté, Dante lives intensely the drama of the impossible direct dialogue with divine reality. If the transformation of this drama into a poetic triumph has been its greatest claim to glory, it is nonetheless evident in the last canto of the *Commedia* that ultimate failure awaits the believer and "geometrician" whose eager gaze is fixed on the impossible demonstration, as "high fantasy" collapses and Dante is absorbed into the divinity unattainable by the exercise of human reason. And is not the assumption of the role of protagonist (the poet as hero) the confirmation of the crisis of the Christian epic? It is as if Homer or Virgil were to make himself the hero of his own classic epic, merely because he has tried to chronicle it. But for Dante the true epic is inseparable from its celebration; the journey is one with the story he makes of it. The poet is the hero.

Let us think once more of the problem of *truth* in Dante's poem—a truth that is translatable only through fable, because its ultimate essence pertains to God. What reaches us is the mythopoetic, classical-evangelical disguise; hence it is a truth forced to change into a *lie* in order to become comprehensible, since the language of God is alien to us, His metaphor spent. It seems to me indeed strange that in the famous image of the universe as a book written by God one should be required to see proof of the medieval and Dantean optimism in relation to the divine, when instead this image expresses the supreme point of a gnosiological despair. For who could ever decipher the divine language, more obscure and inaccessible than Egyptian hieroglyphs are to us? Who could ever trace the meaning behind the syntactical intricacy and lexical preciosity of the Sublime Grammarian?

Dante, then, is following in the footsteps of Saint Thomas, trying to persuade himself and others of the need for a multiple and sacral reading of his own work; in other words, he is trying to represent his poem as a sacred work, a new Scripture in which both heaven and earth have had a hand. For even according to Saint Thomas, the Sacred Story is the sole narrative in which the literal meaning is never in question; hence, if Dante's poem is "sacred," what he relates is true by definition. Dante does not forget that for Saint Thomas pure and simple poetic expression "non supergreditur modum litteralem" (does not go beyond the literal level), and that the Christian art introduced after the writing of the Scriptures has a parabolic rather than an allegorical value; the latter pertains, only to the work inscribed by God. Therefore, in the *Letter to Can Grande* he enumerates all the various meanings of the poem—literal, allegorical, moral, and anagogical—which constitute the same strata of meanings earlier specified by Saint Thomas for the Bible. He then tells us that in the exodus of the Israelites from Egypt we are also to see the "exitus anime sancte ab huius corruptionis servitute ad eterne glorie libertatem," (the conversion of the soul from the sorrow and misery of sin to a state of Grace) (par. 7); and here there is no problem, as the episode is considered true in all senses, even the historical-literal.

But, then, what of Geryon—and also of the whole assemblage of classical-mythological apparitions in the *Commedia*? Does not Dante remember having distinguished in the *Convivio* between the "hidden verity beneath the beautiful lie" typical of pagan poets, and the sacred Scriptures, true in every sense, from the literal to the anagogical? There can be no doubt that he remembers, but meanwhile he has begun writing the *Commedia* and understands his problem as the delineator of the Christian afterworld. He knows that he stands alone with his literary memories and philosophical culture, and that he is in the situation described in the last paragraphs of the *Letter to Can Grande,* where he cites Saint Paul's statement in the Epistle to the Corinthians: "et vidit arcana Dei, che non licet homini loqui." (and I saw the mysteries of God, which are not lawful for a man to utter). Whether he has seen these "hidden things" or not, once he has decided to speak of them the real problem appears, that of language:

Vidit ergo, ut dicit, aliqua "que referre nescit et nequit rediens." Diligenter quippe notandum est quod dicit "nescit et nequit": nescit quia oblitus, nequit quia, si recordatur et contentum tenet, sermo tamen deficit. Multa namque per intellectum videmus quibus signa vocalia desunt: quod Plato satis insinuat in suis libris per assumptionem metaphorismorum: multa enim per lumen intellectuale vidit que sermone proprio nequivit exprimere. [par. 29]

He saw, then, as he says, certain things "which he who returns has neither knowledge nor power to relate." Now it must be carefully noted that he says "has neither knowledge nor power"—Knowledge he has not, because he has forgotten; power he has not, because even if he remembers and retains it thereafter, nevertheless speech fails him. For we perceive many things by the intellect for which language has no terms—a fact which Plato indicates plainly enough in his books by his employment of metaphors; for he perceived many things by the light of the intellect which his everyday language was inadequate to express. [*The Letters of Dante,* transl. Paget Toynbee, 1966, pp. 209-210]

Not only Saint Paul, then, but Plato too is quoted, hardly an authority on Christian faith. This is an implicit indication that the whole poem is to be read as *metaphor.* In order to reveal the truth, Dante is obliged to adopt the lie of the ancient poets, even to use their inventions. The appearance of Geryon brings into focus Dante's assumption of the role of a Christian Orpheus.

The problem of why language should occupy a central position in Dante's philosophical and poetic work is therefore understandable. The language that can reach God, or speak of God, does not exist; indeed, the very fact that man must have recourse to the word is evidence of his predicament. Consequently language is the tangible proof of human decadence, yet is presented as an "egregium humani generis actum" (so excellent an act of the human race) (*De vulgari eloquentia,* I, iv, 3)—a statement already rife with humanistic pride. This is the same ambivalent attitude that Dante entertains toward reason, man's glory and symbol of his sinful state (the angels have no need of it), that reason which always has something fraudulent about it, as does language, its favorite weapon.

And now the complexity of the Dantean problem is revealed, the knot at the center of all his striving for a poetic-rational construction. He has nothing but language with which to address God, yet he knows that the only way really to enter into contact with reality lies in a realm where the human word cannot penetrate the surface and from which man is excluded, at least in this earthly life. How then can one speak of God and of His world if language does not exist in that world? Not only angels, but even devils and the damned have no need to speak (*De vulgari eloquentia*, I, ii, 4): all that has passed from mortal life is, by definition, quit of human stammering. How then define a work that from its very first attempts fails to discover a language adapted to its theme, for the simple reason that none exists? Dante has an answer to this question; if we follow the text of the poem, instead of allowing ourselves to be distracted by the *Letter to Can Grande*, the explanation appears right in the middle of the Geryon episode, where he reveals how complex and vexatious is his relation to the art of language. This work of which we are speaking, Dante's work, is now termed "comedy": "I swear to you by the notes of this Comedy." Several cantos later, Virgil defines his *Aeneid* as "high tragedy"; the definition helps us to understand how Dante, at least in his poem, is outside the range of the Aristotelian classification of literary genres and here ascribes to the terms "comedy" and "tragedy" a personal and original meaning. According to the traditional definition, accepted elsewhere by Dante, tragedy is superior to comedy as a literary genre:

> Per tragediam superiorem stilum inducimus, per comediam inferiorem.... Stilo equidem tragico tunc uti videtur, quando cum gravitate sententie tam superbia carminum quam constructionis elatio et excellentia vocabulorum concordat. [*De vulgari eloquentia*, II, iv, 5, 7]

> By tragedy we bring in the higher style, by comedy the lower style.... We appear then to make use of the tragic style when the stateliness of the lines as well as the loftiness of the construction agree with the weight of the subject. [*Translation of the Latin Works by Dante Alighieri*, transl. A. G. Ferrers, 1904, pp. 78–79]

Inherent in this concordat is the idea that is to ripen in the poem and that will define Dante's own work as comedy. A tragedy is a work in which language succeeds in fully expressing the theme it means to present: it is a work whose nobility of expression *accords with* the sublimity of its content. Therefore Virgil is right in defining his own poem as tragedy, because Aeneas' deeds accord with the language of the Latin epic. And Dante is equally right in defining his poem as comedy, because his comedy, in contrast to a tragedy, is a work whose language is entirely inadequate to express the reality the author wishes to represent and thus is in a state of perpetual failure which no human effort can rectify. The *divine tragedy* has been delineated in that mysterious unwritten alphabet employed by God's angels, whereas Dante has only human language with which to describe the supernatural world, and his poem, in the eyes of God, can only be comedy, a valorous yet pitiable parody of His supreme, unwritten tragedy.

If this interpretation corresponds to the truth, it is understandable why, in the Geryon episode, Dante presents the reader with such a definition of his work, a definition charged with both humility and pride. Let us look once more at the situation in which the term "comedy" appears. Dante exhorts the reader to believe him, swearing by his poem, suddenly termed "comedy." He leads us to understand, moreover, that the instant he is not believed, the "notes" of his work will cease to enjoy the favor of his present and future readers, and the entire structure will be in danger of collapsing. At the very moment that Fraud is about to emerge, not only in Dante's consciousness but before the reader's eyes, the poet again views his work as a lie, an inadequate web of words, a fresh pathetic challenge by Arachne to Minerva. At the same time he speaks in the name of truth, and this is where he differs from Geryon: Do not doubt, reader, that I fervently serve the truth, despite appearances; read my story in depth, and find the ultimate meaning of this journey in quest of reality.

Therefore Geryon, the aerial fish who overcomes the obstacle of the abyss, looses the entangled anchor that impedes the journey and takes the pilgrim on his back, down to Malebolge, where Geryon, "disburdened of our persons, vanished like an arrow from the string" (*Inferno*, XVII, 135–136). Here, in this world devoid of sky and sea, where fish and bird exchange roles according to the fluctuations of a terrifying internal geography and a concomitant view of events, we witness the double nature of the beast—through Dante's anxious eyes looking downward during the descent, or those of the falconer turned upward in expectation of the thwarted predator's return. The image of the beast-falcon without prey after the descent alludes, this time quite clearly, to its defeat. Geryon has been reduced by Virgil and Dante to a mere tool. Fraud has been defrauded.

From the very beginning of the poem, Dante had faced the difficulty of narration:

> Ahi quanto a dir qual'era è cosa dura
>   esta selva selvaggia e aspra e forte.
>
> > [*Inferno*, I, 4–6]

Ah, how hard it is to tell what that wood was, wild, rugged, harsh.

"How hard it is to tell . . ."—the autobiography of the work is here made explicit. But also throughout the *Commedia* Dante obliquely refers to the obstacles encountered by the work in progress. The symbolism of the first canto should be reviewed from this angle of interpretation. The wood, for instance, unquestionably represents sin, but is also the symbol of the predicament of creation. The poet seeks to overcome it by scaling the "hill" illuminated by the rays of the sun. This hill, I believe, represents Parnassus, and the climbing of it is a true *gradus ad Parnassum*, the mount sacred to the Muse and consecrated to Phoebus, charioteer of the sun and patron of the poetic arts. If my interpretation is valid, the attempt to climb Parnassus is a reference to the works written by Dante between the time of his exile and his writing of the *Commedia*, particularly the *Convivio*.

As he begins his ascent, Dante's way is impeded by the three beasts, and he is forced back "to where the sun is silent." Here the autobiography of the work is united with the allegorical-moral meaning. Dante meets Virgil, and at first they speak only of poetry: "Why do you not climb the delectable mountain?" Virgil asks (I, 77). Later he points out the way to descend as a necessary preliminary to the ascent. Now Dante understands that the poetic endeavor will not be fruitful until he is inspired by a regeneration of his whole being. There begins the singular adventure of a man who feels capable of fully realizing his own Christian faith only through becoming a great poet, and of becoming a great poet only through fervently embracing the religious inspiration because of the expressive possibility it offers him.

Another impressive demonstration of the "necessity of belief" in order to achieve poetic supremacy is provided in Canto IX of the *Inferno*, when Virgil and Dante are shut out of the city of Dis and are waiting for the divine messenger to come and open the gates. The two poets are literally stuck in a situation of siege; the return to God is momentarily impeded. On the summit of the highest tower of Dis three Furies appear and invoke the coming of Medusa (or Gorgon), the mythologic pagan deity who has the power of turning to stone whoever gazes on her face. Virgil hastens to warn Dante:

> "Volgiti 'n dietro e tien lo viso chiuso;
>   chè se 'l Gorgòn si mostra e tu 'l vedessi,
>   nulla sarebbe di tornar mai suso."
>
> Così disse 'l maestro; ed elli stessi
>   mi volse, e non si tenne a le mie mani,
>   che con le sue ancor non mi chiudessi.
>
> [IX, 55–60]

"Turn your back, and keep your eyes shut; for should the Gorgon show herself and you see her, there would be no returning above." Thus said the master, and he himself

turned me round and, not trusting to my hands, covered my
face with his own hands as well.

Then, as happens frequently at the most intense moments of
the work's autobiography, Dante addresses the reader:

O voi ch'avete li 'ntelletti sani,
   mirate la dottrina che s'asconde
   sotto 'l velame de li versi strani.

[IX, 61–63]

O you who have sound understanding, mark the doctrine
that is hidden under the veil of the strange verses!

Let us accept this invitation. But let us first consider that Dis is
the city of "heretics" who, according to Dante's definition, are
those sinners who do not believe in the immortality of the soul;
we would call them atheists today. Among them Dante will find
Cavalcante Cavalcanti, the father of Guido Cavalcanti, a poet
and close friend. And Cavalcante asks him:

    "Se per questo cieco
carcere vai per altezza d'ingegno,
   mio figlio ov'è? e perchè non è teco?"
E io a lui: "Da me stesso non vengo:
   Colui ch'attende là, per qui mi mena,
   forse cui Guido vostro ebbe a disdegno."

[X, 58–63]

"If you go through this blind prison by reason of high
genius, where is my son, and why is he not with you?"
   And I to him, "I come not of myself. He who waits yonder
is leading me through here to someone whom perhaps your
Guido had in disdain."

Here I was obliged to correct Singleton's otherwise admirable
translation, which reads: "He who waits yonder, whom perhaps

your Guido had in disdain, is leading me through here." (John Ciardi's translation renders the original text in the same way.) *Cui,* at line 63, means "to someone whom," and does not refer to Virgil but to Beatrice, the figure of Christian revelation, *disdained* by Guido, who, like his father, was an atheist. Dante is saying: It is true that Guido is endowed with a genius comparable to mine, but, being a nonbeliever, he cannot experience this spiritual adventure. And since he cannot experience it, he will not be able to relate it, and his genius will be unfulfilled. When Virgil earlier urged Dante to turn his back to Medusa, symbolically he was warning him to resist the intellectual temptation of the philosophy of an *esprit fort,* typified by his friend, the most admired contemporary poet. Such a philosophy could only bring Dante to a spiritual and poetic stalemate, allegorized in the siege of Dis.

Thus, even the Greek and Latin classics, which could hardly celebrate the Christian hereafter, can be not only imitated and equaled, but even surpassed. Poetic artifices (the journey, the three beasts, the encounters and dialogues with the dead, and so forth) become the necessary instruments for attaining moral truth. But only in the Geryon episode does Dante seem to become fully conscious of his own procedures and of the need to disguise them.

If Geryon is necessary—that is, if the fable and the lie are indispensable to the poet—then writing of God's realm can only produce a comedy. Not comical and not farcical, the gay or grotesque moments in the poem have nothing to do with its title; the title pertains rather to the incorrigible comedy of human language which conduces to parody, without intent to blaspheme God and his world. Now Dante has indicated to the reader how he should consider the poem as a work in which the poet is compelled to resort to the "face of a lie" in order to reach the "truth." The first important step has been taken. The second (and last) time Dante uses the word "comedy" is at the beginning of Canto xxi of the *Inferno.*

Così di ponte in ponte, altro parlando
   che la mia comedìa cantar non cura,
   venimmo.

[XXI, 1-3]

(Thus from bridge to bridge we came along, talking of things of which my Comedy is not concerned to sing.)

What had Dante and Virgil been speaking of in the preceding canto? Indeed, it was less a dialogue than a long monologue by Virgil. We are in the pouch of the soothsayers; at the beginning of Canto XX, Dante's courage fails him at the spectacle of the contorted bodies, their faces turned backward. The poet weeps, and Virgil severely rebukes him, urging him to look at the ancient seers and diviners Amphiaraus, Tiresias, Aruns. From that moment Virgil speaks almost without pause. Inflamed by the sight of so many personages known to classic myth and culture, he reaches the highest state of excitement on seeing Manto, the mythical founder of his native city.

E quella che ricuopre le mammelle,
   che tu non vedi, con le trecce sciolte,
   e ha di là ogni pilosa pelle,

Manto fu, che cercò per terre molte;
   poscia si puose là dove naqu'io;
   onde un poco mi piace che m'ascolte.

[XX, 52-57]

And she that covers her bosom, which you cannot see, with her loose tresses, and has on that side all her hairy parts was Manto, who searched through many lands, then settled in the place where I was born—and on this I would have you hear me for a little.

87

"Onde un poco mi piace che m'ascolte" is an exordium entirely in order, and Virgil will speak as a poet to a Dante turned listener. The remainder of the canto belongs to the master, who extemporizes a veritable solo. The passage relating to Manto is like an episode from the *Aeneid* translated into Dantean language. Like the Geryon episode, this too is introduced by an aqueous presence, but one quite different from the sinister and chaotic waters of Phlegethon, which fall unseen into the abyss of Malebolge. The description of Lake Garda is precise, visual, topographical:

> Suso in Italia bella giace un laco,
>   a pie de l'Alpe che serra Lamagna
>   sovra Tiralli, c'ha nome Benaco.
> Per mille fonti, credo, e più si bagna
>   tra Garda e Val Camonica e Pennino
>   de l'acqua che nel detto laco stagna.
> Loco è nel mezzo là dove 'l trentino
>   pastore e quel de Brescia e 'l veronese
>   segnar poria, s'e' fesse quel cammino.
> Siede Peschiera, bello e forte arnese
>   da fronteggiar Bresciani e Bergamaschi,
>   ove la riva 'ntorno più discese.
>
>   [xx, 61-72]

Up in fair Italy, at the foot of the mountains that bound Germany above Tirol, lies a lake which is called Benaco. By a thousand springs, I think, and more, the region between Garda and Val Camonica and Pennino is bathed by the water which settles in that lake, and in the middle of it is a spot where the pastors of Trent and Brescia and Verona, if they went that way, might give their blessing. Peschiera, a beautiful and strong fortress to confront the Brescians and the Bergamese, sits where the shore around is lowest.

It is a *classical* landscape, without mystery, where every element is precisely ordered. This water too rises at many points and flows downward, not with blind force but with the joyous plenitude of fecundity, till it settles in the marsh, where the eye of him who describes it has followed every stage of its course.

> Ivi convien che tutto quanto caschi
>   ciò che'n grembo a Benaco star non può,
> e fassi fiume giù per verdi paschi.
> Tosto che l'acqua a correr mette co,
>   non più Benaco, ma Mencio si chiama
> fino a Govèrnol, dove cade in Po.
> Non molto ha corse, ch'el trova una lama,
>   nella qual si distende e la 'mpaluda;
> e suol di state talor esser grama.

[xx, 73–81]

(There all the water that in the bosom of Benaco cannot stay must descend and make itself a river, down through green pastures. Soon as the water starts to run, it is no longer named Benaco, but Mincio, as far as Govèrnolo, where it falls into the Po; and after a short course it comes to a level where it spreads and makes a marsh that sometimes in summer is unwholesome.)

Into the next passage Manto is introduced, the "cruel virgin" who chooses the marshy plain as a theater for the practice of her arts; after her death, those who founded the city, choosing the place for defensive reasons ("because of the marsh it had on all sides"), called it Mantua, in memory of the sorceress ("for her who first chose the place").

> Però t'assenno che, se tu mai odi
>   originar la mia terra altrimenti,
> la verità nulla menzogna frodi.

[xx, 97–99]

> Therefore I charge you, if you ever hear other origin given to my city, let no falsehood defraud the truth.

Here again the words "truth" and "falsehood" appear, and again at a crucial point. What was Virgil trying to prove by his long digression? It seems to me improbable that this was a criticism of the fables, as has been asserted by certain modern commentators. A truly Christian criticism would have begun by casting doubt on the entire story of the sorceress—indeed, on her very existence—as the figment of a false, delusive religion. But how is it possible to deny the existence of Manto when her soul is there before them in this inferno as seen by Dante, peopled with deceptions that must serve to render it comprehensible to man? And charging the scene with irony is the fact that Manto's existence is not real for Dante in the same way it is for Virgil, and that the adjective "real" does not have the same weight for the two poets. If in fact, as seems probable, one of Virgil's reasons for recounting this story is to free the founding of Mantua from any suspicion of magic (and thus himself from the reputation of soothsayer, which had clung to him throughout the Middle Ages), his way of relating the story, apparently objective, becomes positively ambiguous, and the ambiguity does not escape Dante. We are in the presence of one of those merciless yet disguised verbal duels that play an important part in the relations between the two, and in which Dante's skill is equal to Virgil's.

As for the story of Manto, what knowledge could Virgil have had of what actually happened? What, in fact, was the source of his information on the origins of Mantua? Certainly not the Christian God, who would not have told him such an absurd tale of sorceresses and other mythological agents; hence the story is an arrant lie or a pretty fable. To try to rectify the *Aeneid* (in which the founding of the city is traced to Ocno, Manto's son) in order to arrive at this new conclusion raises the question: How can Virgil have deluded himself for so long? Such a delusion seems highly preposterous to Dante; when, at the end of his story, Virgil uses the words "truth" and "falsehood," Dante does his utmost to remain serious:

E io: "Maestro, i tuoi ragionamenti
   mi son sí certi prendon sḿia fede,
   che li altri mi sarien carboni spenti.
Ma dimmi, de la gente che procede,
   se tu ne vedi alcun degno di nota;
   ché solo a ciò la mia mente rifiede."

[xx, 100-105]

And I, "Master, your words are to me so certain and do so hold my confidence, that all others would be to me as dead coals. But tell me, of the people who are passing, if you see any that are worthy of note, for to that alone does my mind revert."

In short, Dante is saying: Let us pass on to something else; otherwise I might be in danger of making comments displeasing to the master. One would be that we are in the canto of the soothsayers, and that if Virgil wishes to divest himself of his dubious reputation it is not very wise of him to relate, or rather fabricate, spurious tales, *to divine the past* like a soothsayer—that is to say, a poet, a living distortion who "looks behind and makes his way backwards," like the damned of that *bolgia*. Now Dante's tears at the beginning of the canto become more understandable, as does the harsh, otherwise unjustified rebuke from Virgil, who has understood why his disciple gives way to despair. Dante is telling us: These tortured souls are "our image," we poets, prophets, and liars. And you too, reader, understand very well what I wish to say and am unwilling clearly to express:

Se Dio ti lasci, lettor, prender frutto
   di tua lezione, or pensa per te stesso
   com'io potea tener lo viso asciuto,
quando la nostra imagine di presso

> vidi sì torta, che 'l pianto de li occhi
> le natiche bagnava per lo fesso.
> Certo io piangea, poggiato a un de' rocchi
> del scuro scoglio.
>
> [xx, 19–26]

Reader, so God grant you to take profit of your reading, think now for yourself how I could keep my cheeks dry when near at hand I saw our image so contorted that the tears from the eyes bathed the buttocks at the cleft. Truly I wept, leaning on one of the rocks of the hard crag.

These tears would manifest the dread of a possible accusation directed against the spirit animating not only the *Aeneid* but the *Commedia* as well, both works in which the future is foretold with consummate assurance and the past reshaped with calculated sorcery.

If the art of the poet is to *divine the past,* Virgil can go on recounting his fables for as long as he likes; they will never convince Dante. Yet the disciple concurs with him completely, since Manto is present with the other mythological personages as if she had actually existed and gone to the Christian hell. But Dante is not content to feign belief in these fine mythological stories simply to avoid displeasing Virgil; he makes abundant use of them himself, though he is persuaded to do so only after due consideration, acceding to a strategy of truth that has to undergo the tactical expedients of the lie. The distinction that Virgil makes among the various versions of the Manto story cannot help but evoke Dante's irony. In reality, they are *all* false; the truth is in something other than these, and the *Aeneid* cannot tell it, that "high Tragedy" referred to with pride by Dante's master a few verses later:

> Euripilo ebbe nome, e così 'l canta
> l'alta mia tragedìa in alcun loco:
> ben lo sai tu che la sai tutta quanta.
>
> [xx, 112–114]

Eurypylus was his name, and thus my high Tragedy sings of
him in a certain passage—as you know well, who know the
whole of it.

Virgil has consented to exhibit yet another soothsayer; before
turning to Dante's contemporaries, he lingers with particular
satisfaction on the figure of Eurypylus, already celebrated in the
Aeneid not as a seer but as the bearer of an oracular response.
This is the second time that Virgil corrects himself, and here
perhaps the correction is merely a lapse and of no special significance. It does not escape Dante, however, who puts into Virgil's
mouth the ironic words: "as you know well, you who know the
whole of it." If Dante knows the whole of it, then he knows that
Eurypylus is not a seer; so what is he doing in hell?
   We have arrived at the word "tragedy," and it has required the
mythological-fabulous introduction to give Virgil the necessary
incentive of pride to use such a term—"high Tragedy," to be
sure. Concerned with this world and the events which for Virgil
are real even now when he has been sent by Beatrice to guide
Dante to the otherworld, the Latin poet recovers a majesty and
sureness of tone that derive from the conviction of having recounted the right things in the right way. And here we note an
aspect of the split in the character-Virgil which should be ex-
plored more deeply: the Virgil who defines his own gods as
"false and lying" (*Inferno*, I, 72) is not the same Virgil who shows
the figures of Manto and Eurypylus. The first is Beatrice's messenger who repeats the lessons he has learned; the second is the
poet of the *Aeneid* who speaks of things he believes in. "My high
Tragedy"—agreed. But what then will Dante's work be, now that
the later poet knows that there are lies which he is constrained to
use? What should it be if not, precisely, "comedy"?

Così di ponte in ponte, altro parlando
   che la mia comedia cantar noncura
   venimmo.

[XXI, 1–3]

93

(Thus from bridge to bridge we came along, talking of things of which my Comedy is not concerned to sing.)

Dante has allowed a brief astute interval to elapse between the words "Tragedy" and "Comedy" in order to avoid a sharp antithesis which, in any case, is not his intention. In the face of Virgil's pride his own might seem a gesture of humility, but if it is humility, it is certainly not in relation to Virgil. For all that his master may believe he has created "Tragedy," the highest aspiration of every poet, the fact remains that Virgil's conviction is based on an illusion of the reality of those fables which Dante knows to be false, concocted out of a reservoir of archetypal wisdom but devoid of factual truth. Dante seems to be saying: If, then, to be defined as tragedy, to find a harmony between language and content, a work must seriously and not tactically concern itself with these things, then better "my Comedy"; of certain things my work "is not concerned to sing." What pride there is in this affirmation! Yes, it is "Comedy," for such it is in the eyes of God; moreover, it far surpasses any "Tragedy," putative or genuine. In fact, it will be Dante, not Virgil, who in paradise will embark on the ultimate poetic voyage. And if the fables can facilitate the journey, they are welcome, since in any case there is nothing to be lost; what difference can a lie make one way or another when every word is a parody of the one, unutterable truth?

So Dante emerges victorious from the disguised duel with his master. That it is a question of a duel is confirmed by other episodes in the poem in which a poetic confrontation serves to affirm the *prouesse* of the narrator-protagonist. The frequent military and courtly terminology of the *Commedia* shows that Dante regards his journey as the return of a deserter or a lost soldier to friendly territory. First it is necessary to pass through enemy ranks, down through the circles of hell, then through the troops of purgatory who are also waiting to be introduced into the court of "the Emperor who reigns there-above" (*Inferno*, I, 124). Situations and terms typical of military life occur repeatedly throughout the poem: the siege of the city of Dis, the grotesque parade of demons in Canto XXI of the *Inferno;* the definition of Virgil and Statius as "grand marshals," of Saint Dominic and Saint Francis as "champions" in the army of Christ, of Beatrice as an "admiral," and of Saint Peter a "baron." On the journey of the paladin-Dante to the celestial court, duels with past and present poets assume a particular significance, whether elucidated or not. But whereas each of the contemporary poets (Forese, Bonagiunta da Lucca, and Guinizzelli) initiates a simulated competition with Dante that is immediately resolved by a declaration of their inferiority in comparison to him, those formidable antagonists, the classical poets, are hardly confronted on the battlefield. Let us take the four poets who receive Dante and Virgil in limbo. The only one not cited again in the poem is Horace, who is called "Satyr" by Dante—that is, author of sermons in verse. That confrontation will be settled outside the *Commedia* in letters written in Latin by Dante. Ovid and Lucan are met squarely and defeated in a contest consisting of descriptions of metamorphoses in which Dante emerges as the victor.

> Taccia Lucano omai là dov' e' tocca
> del misero Sabello e di Nasidio,
> e attenda a udir quel ch'or si scocca.
> Taccia di Cadmo e d'Aretusa Ovidio,
> ché se quello in serpente e quella in fonte
> converte poetando, io non lo 'nvidio;
> ché due nature mai a fronte a fronte
> non trasmutò sì ch'amendue le forme
> a cambiar lor matera fosser pronte.
>
> [*Inferno,* XXV, 94–102]

Let Lucan now be silent, where he tells of the wretched Sabellus and of Nasidius, and let him wait to hear what now comes forth. Concerning Cadmus and Arethusa let Ovid be silent, for if he, poetizing, converts the one into a serpent and the other into a fountain, I envy him not; for two na-

95

tures front to front he never so transmuted that both forms
were prompt to exchange their substance.

Homer, the poet "who, like an eagle, soars above the rest"
(*Inferno,* IV, 96), is confronted indirectly through Dante's encounter with Ulysses in Canto XXVI of the *Inferno;* there is an
implicit comparison between the two journeys, Ulysses' cata-
strophic voyage and Dante's victorious one. The duel between
Dante and Homer is indirect, as indirect as was Dante's knowledge of Homer; in fact, the episode recounted by Ulysses is a
late, post-Homeric elaboration of the hero's adventures. It is
clear, however, that for Dante, as later for the men of the Renaissance, the classics are the true touchstones; it is also clear
that his battle will be completely won only in the *Paradiso.* The
description of paradise is a feat that sets the seal on his superiority as an artist.

One sees how Dante passes over his more troublesome prede-
cessors in silence: Giacomino da Verona, who, though a medi-
ocre poet, had already conceived the idea of describing the
Christian hereafter, and therefore cast a shadow on Dante's
glory; the Arab poets, whom he knew through Brunetto
Latini—a precise knowledge he carefully disguised for other
reasons (a sacred poem of Christianity inspired by the para-
disaical visions of Muslim poets!). Plato had said in *Phaedrus*
that the vision and description of the empyrean are beyond
human powers. This declaration does not hold true for Dante,
however, the only one who has succeeded in such a venture. And
this is the reason why he does not encounter a single poet, classic
or contemporary, in paradise. He stands alone, the "Emperor's"
unvanquished champion.

As for Virgil, he remains Dante's moral and spiritual guide
until the end of the *Purgatorio.* But the poetic confrontation
between the two is enacted in the episode we have analyzed; as
always, Dante has no doubt about his own victory, even though
he refrains from proclaiming his certainty. He is well aware of
the perils of his course:

Così di ponte in ponte, altro parlando
  che la mia comedìa cantar non cura,
  venimmo; e tenavamo 'l colmo, quando
restammo per veder l'altra fessura
  di Malebolge e li altri pianti vani;
  e vidila mirabilmente oscura.
Quale ne l'arzanà de' Viniziani
  bolle l'inverno la tenace pece
  a rimpalmare i legni lor non sani,
ché navicar non ponno—in quella vece
  chi fa suo legno novo e chi ristoppa
  le coste a quel che più vïaggi fece;
chi ribatte da proda e chi da poppa;
  altri fa remi e altri volge sarte;
  chi terzeruolo e artimon rintoppa—:
tal, non per foco ma per divin' arte,
  bollia la giuso una pegola spessa,
  che 'nviscava la ripa d'ogna parte.

[Inferno, XXI, 1–18]

Thus from bridge to bridge we came along, talking of things of which my Comedy is not concerned to sing, and we had reached the summit, when we stopped to see the next cleft of Malebolge and the next vain lamentations: and I saw it strangely dark.

As in the Arsenal of the Venetians, in winter, the sticky pitch for caulking their unsound vessels is boiling, because they cannot sail then, and instead, one builds his ship anew and another plugs the ribs of his that has made many a voyage, one hammers at the prow and another at the stern, this one makes oars, that one twists ropes, another patches jib and mainsail; so, not by fire but by divine art, a thick pitch was boiling there below, which overglued the bank on every side.

Is it not clear? My poetic ship has almost sunk; now it has undergone repair and can continue the voyage. The following two cantos (XXI and XXII) have a gay and jocose tone, quite rare in Dante's poem, as if, after an arduous duel, the author-protagonist were breathing a sigh of relief and celebrating his deliverance from danger.

After Canto XXI the word "comedy" vanishes from the poem; having appeared at the appropriate moment to explain itself, its function is now accomplished. Meanwhile its appearance has rippled the surface of the poem like a seismic movement that is manifested at some distance from its epicenter. At the end of Canto XVIII, the first Malebolge canto, the words "shit" and "Thais the whore" appear; patently comic, such language attempts to show how far it can be distanced from the silence. In the last verse of Canto XXI the devil Malacoda makes a "trumpet of his arse." It is not stylistically contradictory to use in the same poem the word "shit" along with the word "angel," for the distance between these words is of the same order as that between two numbers in an infinite system (in the eyes of God, that is).

The new consciousness of the limits of human expression is responsible for the tremendously heightened realism in Malebolge. Every comparison of the otherworld with basic reality becomes a fresh proof of the inadequacy of language, but at the same time, within its limits, this language reaches its supreme glorification, surpassing all previous conquests. Hence, terrestrial reality wins its paradoxical revenge, encroaching on every simile in a manner ever more vehement and winning so many battles in this war of expression which, waged on the border of the ineffable, is lost at the outset. And that the poet moves on the temporal level of invention is demonstrated by his continual use of simile, the preferred Dantean form of expression, one that Saint Thomas considered unsuited to sacred texts inscribed by God and characteristic rather of the *infima doctrina* of poetic knowledge.

An inferior doctrine presupposes an inferior language—again, that of comedy. Are then the *Purgatorio* and the *Paradiso* also comedy? Unquestionably. The problem remains essentially

the same during Dante's entire journey-narration in the supernatural world. If anything, it is continually augmented by new
difficulties of expression, which, in the poet's eyes, underscore
the ever increasing *comedic* character of his endeavor, until the
final admission:

> Ormai sarà piu corta mia favella,
>> pur a quel ch'io ricordo, che d'un fante
>> che bagni ancor la lingua a la mammella.
>> [*Paradiso*, XXXIII, 106–108]

> Now will my speech fall more short, even in respect to that
> which I remember, than that of an infant who still bathes his
> tongue at the breast.

An infant incapable of speech, or worse—so Dante sees himself,
and not only during the ultimate vision, but throughout the
poem and without a trace of false modesty. Defeat has already
been conceded, especially on beholding the new manifestation
of Beatrice's transcendent radiance:

> Da questo passo vinto mi concedo
>> più che già mai da punto di suo tema
>> soprato fosse comico o tragedo.
>> [*Paradiso*, XXX, 22–24]

> At this pass I confess myself defeated more than ever comic
> or tragic poet was defeated by a point in his theme.

"Comic" and "tragic" are the two adjectives which, according
to conventional categories, define the poets, none of whose subjects has so far transcended them as has Dante's. The glory of a
defeat like his cannot be conceived by orthodox writers of comedy and tragedy. To consider his own work as nothing more
than stammering or whimpering in no way conflicts with his
periodic expressions of pride, since his arrogance relates to man

and his humility to God. Even the characters of his poem who are blessed seem to recognize Dante's problem, and they translate their silence into words, their bliss into laughter, which, like speech, is a purely human attribute, and hence a metaphor for everlasting joy. In the *Paradiso,* to be sure, the word "comedy" is no longer used; the poet prefers the definition "sacred poem," knowing quite well that the two are equivalent, and that anyone who has not understood this should reread the Geryon episode, repeat the necessary journey. If the reader does not undergo the crisis of the abyss, if he does not accept the comedy, he cannot know to what degree the poem is really sacred.

But how could Dante say these things in a letter to Can Grande della Scala, who had asked him to explain that title which was soon to raise doubts in the minds of fourteenth century readers (as is evidenced by the comments of Benvenuto da Imola and Boccaccio)? How could he explain it if the whole meaning of his pursuit is that the reader ought to share his understanding, make the journey with him, each time repeating the adventure of the impossible word that must be spoken? If Dante conceals the true answer within the work itself, it is not because of any vain penchant for literary mystification but because only within the work, the totality of the unfolding experience, can he furnish the interpretive key that is asked of him. Hence the necessity for the critic too to trust the *Commedia* itself rather than other works in which Dante tries to simplify his experience by converting it into something more easily grasped by the contemporary reader. It is hardly surprising that in the tenth paragraph of the Letter to Can Grande he encounters such difficulty that the authenticity of the letter has been periodically questioned because of the flatness of his statements as he endeavors to explain the title of his poem. Here are the arguments derived from academic culture, the diligently reiterated etymologies, the issue of content ("Comedia... differt ergo a tragedia in materia per hoc, quod tragedia in principio est admirabilis et quieta, in fine seu exitu est fetida et horribilis....

Comedia vero inchoat asperitatem alicuius rei, sed eius materia prospere terminatur") and that of language ("Similiter differunt in modo loquendi: elate et sublime tragedia; comedia vero remisse et humiliter"). (Toynbee thus translates these passages: "Comedy . . . differs from tragedy in its subject-matter, in that tragedy at the beginning is admirable and placid but at the end or issue is foul and horrible . . . whereas comedy begins with sundry adverse conditions, but ends happily. . . . Tragedy and comedy differ likewise in their style of language; for that of tragedy is high-flown and sublime, while that of comedy is unstudied and lowly.) And would these lines define Dante's work? Can the *Commedia* be seriously defined as a poem which begins badly and ends well and is written in the language of *muliercule* (women-folk)?

But in paragraph 32 of the same letter the poet makes a revealing remark: "urget enim me rei familiaris angustia" (I am tormented by domestic problems), and adds that he looks to the *magnificentia* (magnificence) of Can Grande for help in order that he may continue to apply himself to these questions. The remark is not only the best evidence for the letter's authenticity (what forger could have conceived of such a statement, and why?) but effectively explains the expository tone, which resembles a *curriculum vitae* in the awkwardness of certain passages and the scholasticism of the whole. Dante undoubtedly was more comfortable reviling the Florentines and the cardinals than trying to prove to Can Grande that he was a man of letters and therefore deserving of help.

But if the letter is in fact Dante's, the stamp of his genius is apparent in the tenth paragraph. Discussing the definition of tragedy and comedy, the poet quotes Horace:

Interdum tamen et vocem comedia tollit,
iratusque Chremes tumido delitigat ore;
et tragicus plerunque dolet sermoni pedestri
Telephus et Peleus."

> Yet sometimes comedy her voice will raise,
> And angrey Chremes scold with swelling phrases;
> And prosy periods oft our ear assail
> When Telephus and Peleus tell their tragic tale

and Dante adds: "et per hoc patet quod Comedia dicit presens opus" (and from this is clear that the present work is to be described as comedy).

From the entire *Ars Poetica* Dante quotes only these lines, which state neither more nor less than that a comedic language may at times conceal a tragic content, and vice versa. What is the intent of this quotation if not to put the reader on guard? Take care, reader, do not trust what I say here; ponder these verses; reflect on why I use them in an apparently inexplicable way; see if by chance they are not applicable to my *Commedia*. And if you suspect that my title conceals something other than what I now say, go back to the poem; I am prepared to guide you on the journey during which the actors of the divine tragedy discuss in human language the pedestrian sermon of our *Commedia*.

4

The Two Poetics of the *Commedia*

An aspect of the autobiography of the work in Dante is the simultaneous presence of two recurrent metaphors within the poem: the explicitly stated image of the work as a ship, and the pervasive, if dissimulated, figure of the work as a plant. It is this affinity-opposition that we shall explore.

The *Commedia*, like the *Odyssey*, is a poem of return and reconquest. Dante too is a wayfaring pilgrim, a shifting point between heaven and earth; he too has a ship which from time to time appears before the proscenium of the poem. It is the ship of poetry which recurs throughout the literature of the Middle Ages, the triumphant vessel that enters the purgatorial canticle:

> Per correr miglior acque alza le vele
> ormai la navicella del mio ingegno,
> che lascia dietro a sé mar sì crudele.
>
> [*Purgatorio*, I, 1–3]

(To course over better waters the little bark of my genius now hoists her sails, leaving behind her a sea so cruel.)

A vehicle of many heroes of the early epic poems, the ship becomes the quintessential symbol of the poetic activity considered as epos in the Middle Ages, until at last, in Dante, a singular substitution of persona is effected—perhaps the end toward which the medieval metaphorizing had long been gravitating. The author of the poem seems to be the seafaring hero, and the poem itself the ship plowing unknown seas:

> O voi che siete in piccioletta barca,
>   desiderosi d'ascoltar, seguiti
>   dietro al mio legno che cantando varca...
>
> [*Paradiso,* II, 1–3]

(O you that are in your little bark, eager to hear, following behind my ship that singing makes her way...)

In Dante, there is always the possibility of a reference to both types of protagonists of the ancient epos: the poet on the one hand, and the voyager on the other. Jason and Ulysses are seen by Dante as progenitors of the *Commedia,* as are Homer and Virgil; for Dante, protagonist of his own poem, is also his own Homer and Ulysses. The boldness with which he uses these images at key points of the poem—the opening lines of the *Purgatorio* and of the *Paradiso*—has the authority of a clarion declaration of poetics; it is the trumpet blare of victory acclaimed, of the epic of poetic creation. If it were possible to separate the Homer from the Ulysses inherent in Dante, this declaration would convey both the exultation of the voyager and the joy of the pilgrim-hero. In the course of his voyage he exclaims: What a ship is this ship of mine, vessel of my genius! And he looks to it as to an instrument, or a craft sufficiently sturdy to carry him to the pinnacle of the heavens.

As a navigator, Dante is pragmatic, employing calendars and stellar clocks to the point of obsession; but he also has the spirit of the seafarer, from the tumultuous ecstasy of setting sail—"ma misi me per l'alto mare aperto" (*Inf.,* XXVI, 100 ["But I put forth on the deep open sea"]); to the melancholy at the close of day—"Era già l'ora che volge il disio / ai navicanti" (*Purg.,* VIII, 1–2 ["It was now the hour that turns back the longing of seafaring folk"]); to hallucinatory visions—"che fè Nettuno ammirar l'ombra d'Argo" (*Par.*, XXXIII, 96 ["that made Neptune wonder at the shadow of the Argo"]).

Ecstasy and pragmatism are qualities that characterize Ulysses, Greek qualities which suggest to Dante all manner of impetus and caution. And the mention of Ulysses evokes in us the episode in the *Odyssey* where the hero builds a raft in order to get away from Kalypso's island. Homer meticulously describes his hero's labors as a carpenter. The wood for the raft is taken directly from live trees which Ulysses fells, trims, and joins. The intensity of the episode makes it apparent that something more than a craftsman's procedures is at issue. Through the medium of his carpentry, Ulysses, *homo-faber* par excellence, manifests the grandeur and the limitations of his attitude toward the knowable world. First there is the Trojan horse, which decides the ten-year war, then the raft, which transports him over the seas to Ithaka. Even the bow that only he can bend is his own handiwork. Each time that he succeeds in reaffirming his mastery, the tree is subdued and transformed. The plant has become a horse, raft, a bow.

Yet there remains a void in the hero's heart, as becomes clear in the crucial scene with Penelope at the end of the poem. Here we learn that, besides his other feats of carpentry, Ulysses has constructed a far more extraordinary work: the bed built from a living tree that is deeply rooted in the courtyard of his house. This is the sole work that did not require the destruction of the living plant; the bed is a phenomenon whose symbolic importance cannot be overemphasized, coming as it does at the end of the poem and when Ulysses is celebrating the culmination of his voyage. Is this then the supreme ambition: to utilize nature without destroying it, to construct a bed that lives on as a tree?

It is perhaps the dream of building with imperishable material that generates the work of art. But even Ulysses' enterprise has its limits; the work of art is part of an already existing vegetation. The real creator, the god, is he who created the root and plant.

The highest dream is to invest the inanimate with a soul, not simply to graft the one onto the other.

In a myth, Daphne, object of Apollo's love, is transformed into a laurel, which becomes the crown of poets and symbol of the creative gift. Here the actors in the drama are simplified, mythologized in fact: the god's desire creates nature, which in turn is utilized by the poet's desire. The poet creates art on a secondary level, as Dante will later affirm. Is human art destined merely to tear from the living plant leaves to adorn the poet's brow, only to hew the trunk of the tree to construct the glorious ship that will traverse Dante's imaginary seas? How is it possible for art to *create* life? The first step toward finding an answer to this question is to perceive the hidden relationship between the plant and the ship in Dante, and this is revealed metonymically through the use of the word *legno*, "wood," for both: "Per le nove radici d'esto legno" (*Inf.*, XIII, 73 ["By the new roots of this tree"]). Here *legno* is the plant; in another line, it is the ship: "dietro al mio legno che cantando varca" (*Paradiso*, II, 3 ["following behind my ship that singing makes her way"]). In both instances there is a deep semantic relation through which the metaphors of the ship and the plant are joined, as if to allude to a similarity of nature.

Elsewhere the voyage of the ship is implicitly associated with the winter of the plant; it is the moment of searching and of expectation.

> ch'i' ho veduto tutto 'l verno prima
> lo prun mostrarsi rigido e feroce,
> poscia portar la rosa in su la cima;
> e legno vidi già dritto e veloce
> correr lo mar per tutto suo cammino,
> perire al fine a l'intrar de la foce.
>
> [*Paradiso*, XIII, 133–138]

for I have seen first, all winter through, the thorn display itself hard and stiff, and then upon its summit bear a rose.

106

And I have seen ere now a ship fare straight and swift over the sea through all her course, and perish at the last as she entered the harbor.

The ship entering the harbor is likened to the plant that finally blooms; both are the joyous outcome of the adversities, of winter and the voyage. There are plants that wither and ships that never reach port, and Dante gives instances of both, in the Pier delle Vigne and the Ulysses episodes. Consider the association of images in the following lines:

che la fortuna che tanto s'aspetta,
   le poppe volgerà u' son le prore,
   sì che la classe correrà diretta;
e vero frutto verrà dopo 'l fiore.

[XXVII, 145–148]

that the storm which has been so long awaited shall turn round the sterns to where the prows are, so that the fleet shall run straight; and good fruit shall follow on the flower.

Here the two images are successfully united; the victorious journey and the phenomenon of vegetation seem to mirror each other. The wood of the ship sails toward the symbolic flowering that awaits it at the port. The plant, transformed into a ship, aspires to return to its living roots, to *become* a plant again. If the work as ship represents the voyage, the challenge, the poetic effort as epic deed, the work as plant represents the biology of creation, the will to create something which, in the fulness of time, can live an autonomous life. The work as plant is the second and most profound of the poetics animating the Dantean poem.

Indeed, the *Commedia*, this ship sailing toward the port of God, seems also to be striving to transform itself into a living plant. This is primarily evident at the metaphorical level. There are no more frequently recurring images in the poem than those of growing plants: seed, root, branch, foliage, flower, and fruit; no aspect of life that is not compared to a botanical phenomenon. Every fundamental human function finds a place in a semantic field dominated by the phenomenology of vegetation. One might say that for Dante this is the prototype, virtually the organic model, of every vital process.

To begin with genealogical transmission: Cunizza da Romano discloses that she is the sister of Ezzelino III by saying, "I and he sprang from the same root" (*Par.*, IX, 31). And Dante's ancestor, Cacciaguida, exclaims, "Oh, my branch . . . I was your root" (XV, 88–89). Dante appositely replies, "O dear root of me" (XVII, 13). Hugh Capet, referring to his descendants, says, "I was the root of the evil plant" (*Purg.*, XX, 43). Sordello, comparing Charles I of Anjou to Charles II, says, "As much is the plant inferior to its seed" (VII, 127). Guido del Duca characterizes Bernardin de Fosco of Faenza in the words "noble scion of a lowly plant" (XIV, 102). And, in another context, "Rarely does human worth rise through the branches" (VII, 121–122). And "How from sweet seed may come forth bitter" (*Paradiso*, VIII, 93). Such references to the degeneration of a family had already appeared in the *Convivio* in another metaphor of vegetation: "for the divine seed [of nobility] falls not upon the race, that is the stock, but falls upon individuals" (IV, XX, 5).

The reader will have noticed that almost none of these images is expressed as a simile; therefore it appears to be natural for Dante to associate the continuation of the human species with the vegetable life form. When he says, "Rarely does human worth rise through the branches, and this He wills who gives it, in order that it may be asked of Him" (*Purgatorio*, VII, 121–123), it is clear that the infrequency of a resemblance between father and son is because the relationship is ephemeral, illusory, fortuitous. The Christian fear of sensuality tends to view procreation as a sort of tithe which the postangelic nature must pay for the privilege of preserving and perpetuating life; thus the blood relationship is of little consequence. Dante's Christianity conceives humanity as a forest in whose common ground man's *true* roots are implanted, and this ground is God. Like a plant, every individual man is essentially isolated in the uniqueness and singularity of his individual soul, which alone defines his physiognomy. The paternal seed and the maternal egg are instruments of the fecundating will of God. The generative model remains the evangelical one of the miraculous birth of Christ, beyond carnal contact, as in Cacciaguida's evocation of his own coming into the world:

> A così riposato, a così bello
>   viver di cittadini, a così fida
>   cittadinanza, a così dolce ostello,
> Maria mi diè, chiamata in alte grida.
>
> [*Paradiso*, XV, 130–133]

> To so reposeful, to so fair a life of citizens, to such a trusty community, to so sweet an abode, Mary, called on with loud cries, gave me.

There exists then an earthly geneaological tree—the family and its issue, the royal house—whose reality is not denied by Dante, but whose importance is minimized in relation to the tree of real life, which isolates every man in a direct and exclusive relationship with the divinity of his own origin. In the forest of humanity, every individual is conceived as a plant that awaits its flowering.

This is perhaps the most telling instance of the vegetation metaphors. Other human functions are assimilated to plant life—above all, language, the mutability of which is remarked by Adam:

> ché l'uso di mortali è come fronda
> in ramo, che sen va e altra vene.
>
> [XXVI, 137–138]

for the usage of mortals is as a leaf on a branch, which goes away and another comes.

And knowledge is represented as a plant, when Saint Peter interrogates Dante:

> E quel baron che sì di ramo in ramo,
>   esaminando, già tratto m'avea,
>   che a l'ultime fronde appressavamo...
>
> [XXIV, 115-117]

And that Baron who, thus from branch to branch examining, had now drawn me on so that we were approaching the last leaves...

Even the desire to know "springs up like a shoot":

> Nasce per quello, a guisa di rampollo,
>   a piè del vero il dubbio.
>
> [IV, 130-131]

Because of this, questioning springs up like a shoot, at the foot of the truth.

Dante also terms true happiness "the good essence, the fruit and root of every good" (*Purg.*, XVII, 134-135). The greatest offense he commits at Florence is to call the city Lucifer's "plant" (*Par.*, IX, 127). Time has its "roots" in the primum mobile and its "leaves" in the other heavens (XXVII, 118-120), and the "will" in men is compared to "sound plums" that the rain of temptation turns into "blighted fruit" (XXVII, 124-126). Referring to his own sin, Guido del Duca remarks, "Of my sowing I reap such straw" (*Purg.*, XIV, 85); and Saint Benedict speaks of the fires of *caritas* as "that warmth which gives birth to holy flowers and fruits" (*Par.*, XXII, 47-48). In the same canto, the confidence acquired by Dante is compared to "the rose when it opens" (XXII, 56), and the duration of good acts to the brief time "from the springtime of the oak to the bearing of the acorn" (XXII, 87).

It is clear, even from a cursory survey, that between the final cantos of the *Purgatory* and the whole of the *Paradiso*, this great metaphorical burgeoning invests every aspect of life. Thus Statius acknowledges the debt which, as a poet, he owes to Virgil's *Aeneid:* "The sparks which warmed me ... were the seeds of my poetic fire" (*Purg.*, XXI, 94–95); the poetic inspiration is a plant of fire. The seed is a moral metaphor when Beatrice solaces Dante with the words, "Lay aside the seed of tears" (XXXI, 46), and is also metaphorically connected to orthodox Christian doctrine as represented by the twenty-four plants in the crown of the blessed in the heaven of the Sun (*Par.*, XII, 95–96). And, finally, the Church: it is a garden, "the catholic garden" (XII, 104) of which Saint Dominic is the "husbandman"; it is also "the vineyard that soon turns gray if the vine-dresser is negligent" (XII, 86–87); and also the "good plant" sown by Saint Peter "which was once a vine and is now become a thorn" (XXIV, 111). The Church, direct intermediary in the human world, is "the field" of the divinity, and God is "the Eternal Gardener" (XXVI, 65). We are reminded of the Rose of the empyrean blessed, or of those two extraordinary angel-plants which descend into the valley of the princes:

> Vedi come fogliette pur mo nate
>   erano in veste, che da verdi penne
>   percosse traen dietro e ventilate.
>
> [*Purgatorio*, VIII, 28–30]

Their robes were green as newborn leaves, which they trailed behind them, smitten and fanned by their green wings.

And Dante compares himself to a "sturdy oak uprooted" by the fury of Beatrice's admonitions (*Purgatorio*, XXXI, 70); the comparison recalls one of the most moving evocations in Dante's work, when, in the *Convivio*, he speaks of plants that have been transformed, and that "either die altogether or live as if in gloom, like things parted from the place dear to them"—a telling image of exile for the uprooted Dante.

The biblical and patristic derivations of this series of metaphors further highlight the semantic system of references to life as a plant. Spiritual life, and poetry too, can wither like a parched tree. Everything has its inception in that "dark wood" of the beginning. Wild, harsh, dense, the vegetable mass is the symbol of a menacing and fatal aridity. And, indeed, the flowering is no more than a hope in the *Inferno*. After Virgil's heartening words, Dante's soul is lifted up like a flower at dawn (*Inferno*, II, 127–130). For the most part, however, the images in the *Inferno* present the harsh and wintry reality of the soul: the souls of the damned are compared to autumnal leaves falling from the boughs (III, 112–116), soul-leaves descending from a "bad seed" to populate the wasteland of the first canto. As always in Dante, the religious dimension is enriched by the aesthetic. The hidden poetics of the plant is first expressed in the botanical metaphor of the Pier delle Vigne episode. We are again in a wood, this time described in obsessive cadences:

> Non fronda verde, ma di color fosco;
>   non rami schietti, ma nodosi e 'nvolti;
>   non pomi v'eran, ma stecchi con tòsco.
>
> [Inferno, XIII, 3–6]

No green leaves, but of dusky hue; no smooth boughs, but gnarled and warped; no fruits were there, but thorns with poison.

Within every plant is concealed a suicide, and cutting one of the branches, Dante elicits a painful reaction from the imprisoned soul. When he hears the story of the poet Pier delle Vigne, who had killed himself in despair because he was unjustly accused, Dante appears to believe in his innocence and condemns him only for the violence done to himself, for his offense against the gift of life. But the moral significance of the episode is secondary to the association of elements created in Dante's imagination: the tree, death, poetry. Here we see the initial paradox of the act of suicide from the Christian viewpoint, the attempt to dispose of a life that ineluctably recurs in the hereafter. The triumph of life over death is the implicit message of every line of the *Commedia;* even the *Inferno* testifies to life's victory, since none of the souls, not even the soul of the suicide, succeeds in releasing himself from life.

Life continues in its ultimate form in the chapter of eternity, and the everlasting winter is mankind's "second death." The *Inferno* is a picture of life transfixed by the impossibility of extension, a permanently truncated existence. In the Christian universe, there is no void: nonexistence can never be attained. This truth must be borne in mind if one is to understand Dante's creative imperative. Every choice of death in life is unfailingly transformed into the choice of a definite form of life in the hereafter. In Pier delle Vigne, Dante is contemplating one of the directions his own destiny might have taken. Pier delle Vigne too was a poet; he too was unjustly accused. But here the resemblance ends, for, in contrast to Dante, he did not redeem his fate through his work. His suicide was merely a short cut to his choice of death over life; the plant that failed to bloom is here the plant of a poetry that failed to find within itself the vitality to build upon unhappiness. Dante's manifest sympathy for the poet reveals how close to the abyss he himself had been—if not to suicide, at least to the temptation to abandon himself to despair, thereby becoming a parched plant for eternity.

Like such a plant would his own work have seemed to Dante had it been curtailed on the eve of the *Commedia,* as had that of Pier delle Vigne. In melancholoy retrospect, the dead poet views his own work as otiose bravura and not worth preserving. Moral judgment is also aesthetic judgment: the poetry of Pier delle Vigne is now and forever the withered plant in the pathless forest like the wood at the opening of the poem. Virgil's active presence is the intermediary between the two later poets; Virgil, who earlier had created a similar situation in the *Aeneid,* bids Dante to break a branch from the tree and first interrogates Pier delle Vigne. Through Virgil, Dante understands and judges the fallen poet—through the model of a poetic work in perennial bloom, the *Aeneid,* the reading of which, according to our interpretation of the first canto of the *Inferno,* has allowed Dante to emerge from the "dark wood" of the creative impasse.

Does it follow then that the ship which does not strive to become a plant is destined to founder? We know that the goal, and hence the flowering, is denied the shade of Odysseus; he is prevented from seeing purgatory, domain of the soul's springtime—a sphere accessible to Dante because he is better attended than the Greek hero. Suddenly a parallelism appears that can hardly be fortuitous. If the opening lines of the first canto celebrate the entry of the poetic bark into "better waters," the closing lines chant the miracle of perennial renewal. The reed plucked from the earth springs up before Dante's astonished eyes.

> Oh maraviglia! ché qual elli scelse
> l'umile pianta, cotal si rinaque
> subitamente la onde l'avelse.
>
> [*Purgatorio,* I, 134–136]

O marvel! that such as he plucked the humble plant, even such did it instantly spring up again, there whence he had uprooted it.

The passage is another Virgilian echo (of *Aeneid,* VI, 143–144), and certainly a moral allegory. This plant, humble yet indestructible, is also the emblem of poetry revived—revived by the spiritual state of inferno, and also in emulation of the great models of the past. It is at this point that Dante's poetry begins its transformation into an indestructible plant; uprooted, it instantly springs up again; forgotten by one reader, it is suddenly brought to life by another.

It is in the *Purgatorio* that the imagery of regeneration is amplified. Between the autumn-winter of the *Inferno* and the radiant summer of the *Paradiso,* the *Purgatorio* stands as a springtime of the soul, "mixing memory and desire"—to borrow T. S. Eliot's phrase. This quality of the *Purgatorio* should not be overlooked; unlike paradise and inferno, which present two absolute seasons sealed in eternity, purgatory is a transitional stage which does not nullify the distinctive quality of earthly experience, its temporality. In purgatory the years are counted, time measured, yet the voyage in eternity has begun; thus purgatory presents a special season that mingles the human with the divine, time with eternity, memory of the earth with the desire for heaven. It is in purgatory that Dante has dreams and visions, which are neither of inferno nor of paradise because bound to temporality and thus to expectation. And while his ship sails the seas of hope, his plant, born as a humble reed, does not cease growing and putting forth leaves.

The vegetative burgeoning of the earthly paradise will be a point of arrival. Before then, and while traveling through the circles of purgatory, Dante experiences the various degrees of development of his poetic plant. Several episodes of the *Purgatorio* are dominated by the image of a tree, and we shall see that each of them is linked to a poet whom Dante encounters and appraises in the light of his own evolution.

The first of these meetings is in Canto XXII of the *Purgatorio,* where, in Statius' speech and Virgil's reply, is found one of Dante's most moving tributes to poetry. Dante the protagonist is exceedingly agitated by the scene. In the tercet immediately preceeding the appearance of the tree, he speaks of himself thus:

Elli givan dinanzi, e io soletto
   di retro, e ascoltava i lor sermoni,
   ch'a poetar me davano intelletto.

[XXII, 127-129]

They were going on in front, and I solitary behind, and I

was listening to their speech which gave me understanding in poetry.

In other words, the discourse between Statius and Virgil gives Dante not only understanding but a desire to create in turn. And suddenly the tree appears.

Ma tosto ruppe le dolci ragioni
   un alber che trovammo in mezza strada,
   con pomi a odorar soavi e buoni;
e come abete in alto si digrada
   di ramo in ramo, cosi quello in guiso,
   cred' io, perché persona sù non vada.
Dal lato onde 'l cammin nostro era chiuso,
   cadea de l'alta roccia un liquor chiaro
   e si spandeva per le foglie suso.

[XXII, 130-138]

But soon the pleasant converse was broken by a tree which we found in the midst of the way, with fruit sweet and good to smell. And as a fir-tree tapers upward from branch to branch, so downwards did that—I think so that none may climb it. On the side where our way was bounded there fell from the high rock a clear water which spread itself over the leaves above.

A voice rises from within the leaves citing examples of temperance (we are now in the circle of the gluttonous); from the standpoint of moral significance, the intent of the episode is quite clear. It is more difficult, however, to understand how Dante ever came to choose a tree, and one so bizarre, through which to convey his message of moderation. Confronted with this image, exegetists have not concealed their difficulty, especially since there soon appears (in Canto XXIV) another tree from which come voices reciting instances of gluttony that have been punished. The tree is described:

parvermi i rami gravidi e vivaci
  d'un altro pomo, e non molto lontani
  per esser pur allora vòlto in laci.
Vidi gente sott' esso alzar le mani
  e gridar non so che verso le fronde,
  quasi bramosi fantolini e vani
che pregano, e 'l pregato non risponde. . . .

[XXIV, 103–109]

the laden and verdant branches of another tree appeared to
me, and not far distant, because only then had I come
round there. Beneath it I saw people lifting up their hands
and crying I know not what toward the leaves, like eager
and fond little children, who beg, and he of whom they beg
answers not.

One of the voices issuing from the tree informs us that its
origin was the tree of the knowledge of good and evil in the
terrestrial paradise; the assertion serves as the basis not only for
the allegorical interpretation of this vegetable image but also for
the earlier one in Canto XXII. Indeed, the two seem to be linked
in such a way that the first tree is made to originate from the tree
in the Garden of Eden and pertains to the admonition against
eating the forbidden fruit. Yet doubt persists in the reader.
What is this tree of the knowledge of good and evil doing in the
circle of the gluttonous and, moreover, in images that duplicate
one another? We may assume that Dante superimposes one
symbolic meaning upon another, the one patently moral, the
other comprising an aesthetic statement.

The problem of interpreting the two plants is insoluble unless
one is disposed to take a comprehensive view of what happens in
the purgatorial cantos. Except for the parenthetical passage in
Canto XXV, which consists of a long philosophical digression by
Statius on the soul and generation, Cantos XXII through XXVI are
composed of Dante's dialogues with poets. There are Statius in
Canto XXII, Forese Donati in Canto XXIII, Bonagiunta da Lucca

and again Forese in Canto XXIV, the philosophical interlude in Canto XXV followed by the entrance into the circle of the lustful in Canto XXVI, and the meeting with Guido Guinizzelli and Arnaut Daniel. *During five entire cantos not a single character appears who is not a poet.* This is a quite remarkable fact which one must consider in every attempt to interpret these episodes.

Beginning with his encounter with Statius, Dante's attention seems to have shifted from the moral plane to that of poetics. He wishes to test his own powers before reaching Beatrice. His encounters with the poets and the images of the two sacred trees symbolize his apprenticeship and his attainment of maturity as a poet. Dante is now equipped to portray paradise, and his meeting with Beatrice and its accompanying rituals will render him morally worthy to ascend to God. True, Dante reaches the terrestrial paradise before the celestial one, Matelda before Beatrice; in other words, he is aesthetically equipped before he is spiritually prepared for the final journey, but only the concurrence of the two states will render him "pure and ready to rise to the stars."

One might ask why Dante did not situate his encounters with the poets in a region outside that of the purgatorial ordeals—in the terrestrial paradise, for example, which only Virgil and Statius succeed in reaching. The answer to this question must take into account Dante's aesthetic strategy rather than his criterion of moral retribution. Virgil and Statius reach the terrestrial paradise (which Matelda also calls Parnassus) because, metaphorically, they had reached it of their own accord and by means of their own poetic works; but no later poet, apart from Dante, has done as much. It is worth remarking that, after Virgil's disappearance from the scene, Dante meets no other poet either in purgatory or in paradise, and this too must be interpreted in the light of his poetics rather than his theology. It suggests that, although no contemporary poet has ever attained the creative height symbolized by Eden-Parnassus, at least in antiquity Virgil and Statius had been capable of reaching it. Relegating Forese,

Bonagiunta, Guinizzelli, and Arnaut Daniel to the purgatorial experience is for Dante the establishment of an artistic hierarchy; it is a declaration that no recent poet has succeeded in making his way to the threshold of Eden-Parnassus, that none has succeeded in emulating the ancients, with the sole exception of Dante, who will surpass them because he will advance beyond Parnassus to paradise. And to all these recent poets he will attribute sins, albeit the most venial of mortal sins, gluttony and lust, in order to adhere to the structure of moral categories in the *Purgatorio*. But the attribution is now secondary to the problem assailing Dante's mind: the legitimization and consecration of his own poetic talent.

Let us consider the two plants not as moral allegories, but as symbols of the creative force that have appeared to him. In the dialogue between Virgil and Statius, Dante listens reverently to "their speech," from which, by his own admission, he gained "understanding in poetry"—At this point, the tree appears, but a tree that stands upside down. Among the many interpretations of this strange plant, the simplest has yet to be offered; it is to be found in Cacciaguida's metaphor for paradise and is the most extraordinary vegetable image of the entire poem:

> ... l'albero che vive de la cima
> e frutta sempre e mai non perde foglia.
>
> [*Paradiso*, xviii, 29–30]

the tree, which has life from its top and is always in fruit and never sheds its leaves.

It is an inverted tree, like the one that appears to Dante as he listens to the discourses of Statius and Virgil. There can be no doubt that the one tree prefigures the other and is intended as an allusion to the attainment of paradise as Dante's supreme exploit; the first tree is manifested to the poet at a moment when he is deeply perturbed and inspired by his predecessor's "speech." The first yield of the new "understanding in poetry" which has flooded Dante's mind, it also presages paradise in symbolic form: an inverted tree with its roots in God.

Dante is, in fact, fascinated by the tree, gazing at it so intently that Virgil gently pleads with him to continue on their way (*Purgatorio*, XXIII, 4–6); the plea suggests that the aspiration to depict paradise before the purgatorial experience has been fulfilled may prove to be an obstacle. The first plant is in close symbolic relation to the presence of Virgil and Statius, and this alone endows it with metaphorical credibility.

The second vision of a tree belongs to a different context. The scene is no longer dominated by the two Latin poets, but rather by poets who are Dante's contemporaries; there is no longer a link between Dante and the poetry of antiquity, but rather a comparison between him and the most esteemed exponents of the poetry of his time. The friendship that Dante feels on meeting these illustrious souls is mixed with a clear perception of the distance separating their respective experiences. That there is a connection between the first and the second tree is equally clear. In the new representation of the tree of poetry, Dante emphasizes still further the difficulty of gathering the fruit of the tree. A voice issuing from the leaves warns him not to approach, as the plant has its origins in the forbidden tree of the terrestrial paradise. The entrance to Eden-Parnassus is thus denied to the poets of Dante's time, who, according to my interpretation, are the individuals referred to as "people lifting up their hands and crying . . . who beg and he of whom they beg answers not" (*Purgatorio*, XXIV, 106–109). If the tree of paradise is prohibited to Statius and Virgil (even though they succeed in evoking it for Dante through the force of their "speech"), the tree of Eden is prohibited to the later poets because none of them has the artistic power to rival the early masters and thereby reach Eden-Parnassus, the first stage of the heavenly ascent. Even from the tree of paradise seen by Statius and Virgil there comes a voice saying, "Of this food you shall have want" (*Purgatorio*, XXII, 141).

And before meeting Beatrice, Dante himself will not be ready for Paradise.

Dante's genius lies in his deep-rooted conviction that heaven is attainable through a poetic masterpiece, and his profound faith rests upon the vast expressive possibilities that the Christian hereafter offers to his imagination. Spiritual evolution can never be separated from its representation. *To believe is to represent,* and vice versa; consequently, spiritual flowering cannot be separated from creative rebirth, and the terrestrial paradise, Eden-Parnassus, is the "forest green and dense" (*Purgatorio,* xxviii, 2) that precedes the summertime of life and art. In the last symbolic plant of the purgatorial canticle the rituals of rebirth are celebrated. The tree appears to the poet during the symbolic procession dominated by the presence of Beatrice.

> Io senti' mormorare a tutti "Adamo";
>   poi cerchiaro una pianta dispogliata
>   di foglie e d'altra fronda in ciascun ramo.
> [Purgatorio, xxxii, 37-39]

I heard "Adam" murmured by all, then they encircled a tree stripped of its flowers and of its foliage in every bough.

The nearer to heaven, the more wide-spread are the branches of the tree, and Dante makes evident that in form it resembles the trees we have already seen. There follows a complex allegorical scene which does not easily yield to a moral interpretation and, like all of the final allegories of the *Purgatorio,* is in part deliberately enigmatic. But there is one element of great metaphorical clarity: the image of the sudden revival of this great plant of Eden, which is at the same time Parnassus—a revival signifying the glorious rebirth of poetic inspiration:

> Come le nostre piante, quando casca
>   giù la gran luce mischiata con quella

> ché raggia dietro a la celeste lasca,
> turgide fansi, e poi si rinovella
>   di suo color ciascuna, pria che 'l sole
>   giunga li suoi corsier sotto altra stella;
> men che di rose e più che di vïole
>   colore aprendo, s'innovò la pianta,
>   che prima avea le ramora sì sole.
>
> [XXXII, 52–60]

As our plants, when the great light falls downward mingled with that which shines behind the celestial Carp, begin to swell, and then renew themselves, each in its own color, before the sun yokes his coursers under other stars; so, disclosing a hue less than of roses and more than of violets, the tree was renewed that first had its branches so bare.

At the end of the canticle, Dante says of himself:

> rifatto sì come piante novelle
> rinovellate di novella fronda.
>
> [XXXIII, 143–144]

(renovated even as new trees renewed with new foliage.)

This then is the conclusion of the *Purgatorio:* the plant of poetry is inseparable from the efflorescence of grace.

The repeated prefiguration of paradise by the purgatorial plant suggests that Dante's great test will come in the third canticle: there his path as pilgrim and as poet will be determined; there, as solitary champion of God, he will seek victory over both the ancient and the contemporary poets; and there he will justify his ambition to be God's sole paladin. The journey to paradise will place the poet-voyager in a new situation. Among Dante's various metaphorical images of God (sun of light and of love, emperor of the celestial court, eternal gardener) is that of supreme artist. In contrast to the human artisan, who works with existing material, God, this most inventive of artists, works with nonexistent material. It is He who created the plant, image of life, He who invented the paradisiac tree. To enter paradise is to enter into God's masterpiece and to portray it with the means afforded by human language. The immense plant is of the same substance as the "great sea of being;" the plant is light, and the sea is of light. Paradise is the universe in which the plant-ship meets it cosmic roots.

There Dante, the human gardener and navigator, confronts the Divine Model. This confrontation is not only an act of faith, but an audacious if subtle and dissimulated challenge. The poetics of the ship, however heroic and sublime is nonetheless a human poetics. The great voyagers Ulysses, Jason, and Aeneas are imitable notwithstanding their relationship to gods; their talent is the human one of acting, transforming, recovering, and connecting, as exemplified in the fabrication of a ship or a bed from a plant. But who can create a plant from nothing? Who can be ambitious enough to prefigure a plant-work, stealing the fire of creation from God? We are no longer astonished by the fact that if in the *Commedia* there is a poetics of the plant-work, it is thoroughly disguised in comparison with that of the ship-work. It is one thing to compete with nature or men, another to compete with God. But in the closing lines of the *Commedia,* when at last he is in God's presence, Dante surrenders. This plant-poem of his, unlike the tree of paradise, cannot live of itself alone. The poem takes on new life at fixed seasons and cannot endure eternally. When will the propitious season, the springtime of the plant return? When a reader resumes reading the poem. If no one were to reopen the *Commedia,* it would wither like Pier delle Vigne's plant. "How briefly lasts the green upon the top," exclaims Oderisi da Gubbio, speaking of the instability of the artist's posthumous fame (*Purgatorio,* xi, 92), and he adds:

> La vostra nominanza è color d'erba,
> che viene e va, e quei la discolora
> per cui ella esce de la terra acerba."
>
> [XII, 115-117]

> Your repute is as the hue of grass, which comes and goes,
> and he discolors it through whom it springs green from the
> ground.

Thus the phenomenon of art follows a cycle analogous to that
of nature. The earth shelters the roots and nourishes the plant,
but it is the sun's warmth that makes possible its renewal and
flowering. The roots of the work are in the poet's soul, but the
reader's love transmits the work from generation to generation.

This Dantean plant never ceases to bloom. A passage from
Dante's great admirer, Ezra Pound, comes to mind:

> Hast 'ou fashioned so airy a mood
> To draw up leaf from the root?

> .   .   .   .   .

> Pull down thy vanity, I say pull down.
> Learn of the green world what can be thy place
> In scaled invention or true artistry.
> Pull down thy vanity. . . .
> The green casque has outdone your elegance.
>
> [*Pisan Cantos,* LXXXI]

Here also the poet sees in the plant a self-sufficient organism
rising to new life, the model of art. And we the readers, remote
in time, are the seasons of the work, Dante's springtime.

5

Macbeth and the Imitation of Evil

Fair is foul, and foul is fair.

—I, i, 11

In the course of his lengthy conclave with the witches (*Macbeth,* IV, i), Macbeth learns that Macduff had fled to England after the murder of Duncan, leaving his castle unguarded, his wife and children defenseless. Macbeth resolves to seize the opportunity to annihilate "His wife, his babes, and all unfortunate souls / That trace him in his line" (ll. 151–152). In the following scene, Macduff's cousin Ross, after trying in vain to calm Lady Macduff's alarm at the news of her husband's flight, leaves her alone with her small son. The brief dialogue between the mother and child is cut short by the arrival of the murderers, who swiftly discharge Macbeth's order to do away with them.

This entire episode is dominated by images of birds and flight. In his use of the verb "to fly," with its secondary meaning "to flee," Shakespeare conveys all he intends to suggest. Used initially in the former sense, gradually the word begins to imply the latter. How can Macduff flee the land, his wife protests, leaving us here defenseless?

> He loves us not,
> He wants the natural touch. For the poor wren,

> The most diminutive of birds, will fight,
> Her young ones in her nest, against the owl.
>
> [IV, ii, 8–11]

Unlike the male bird, Macduff has fled the nest, and it is as if he were dead to his loved ones. "Your father's dead," the mother says to the child after Ross has gone. "And what will you do now? / How will you live?" And the son echoes the New Testament parable: "As birds do, mother. . . . With what I get." Thinking of the pitfalls, of the lime and the net, the mother exclaims: "Poor bird!" (IV, ii, 31–34).

At the opening of the scene, Lady Macduff is certain that her husband's flight was irrational ("His flight was madness") and that he has become a traitor as a result of fear.

> When our actions do not,
> Our fears do make us traitors.
>
> [IV, ii, 3–4]

The words express the contempt reserved for the rash and the cowardly. Ross's unexpected reply is pregnant with meaning:

> You know not
> Whether it was his wisdom or his fear.
>
> [IV, ii, 4–5]

At this juncture, Lady Macduff's amazement is justified. What sort of wisdom or sagacity can possibly underlie Macduff's action? If such there be, she is unable to conceive of it; not even birds leave their nests unprotected. Her attack is so forceful, so explicit, that Ross is again compelled to come to his friend's defense, and in so doing leaves her in no doubt about her plight.

This episode has long been misinterpreted, mainly because it has been considered of secondary significance to Macbeth's great tragedy, whereas in fact it is one of the drama's focal points and decisive for an understanding of the work as a whole.

The essence of Ross's defense of Macduff is in the lines:

> He is noble, wise, judicious, and best knows
> The fits o' th' season.

But having gone thus far, Ross realizes that he cannot prove what he asserts without making a complete revelation, which is proscribed, and adds: "I dare not speak much further." And why not speak? This is not the time to conceal the truth. Ross then makes a slight concession to Lady Macduff's perplexity by adding:

> But cruel are the times, when we are traitors
> And do not know ourselves.

The word "traitors" appears for the second time, here in a context fraught with ambiguity and with at least a partial admission: Macduff may be a traitor, and Ross too perhaps, either unwittingly or feigning lack of awareness. The latter seems more likely; indeed, the haste with which he leaves is, at the very least, suspect:

> I take my leave of you.
> Shall not be long but I'll be here again.

Then, with sinister prescience and foreboding, he declares:

> Things at the worst will cease, or else climb upward
> To what they were before.
>
> [IV, ii, 16–25]

No one takes any action to protect the doomed victims, nor does anyone remain with them. Their fate has been decided; Lady Macduff realizes this at the end of Ross's discourse. If, in fact, Macduff was "judicious," his heedless flight, leaving his castle and family unguarded, would have been unthinkable.

"Fathered he is, and yet he's fatherless," she says of her son, then bluntly says to him: "Your father's dead. / And what will you do now?" He will live "As the birds do," he replies, afterward declaring that his father is not dead. The mother insists that he is, even though she knows he is not. Yet there is something more she wants to say, and sensing it the child inquires: "Was my father a traitor, mother?" (IV, ii, 31–44).

Again the word appears—the third time spoken without hesitation. "That he was," replies the mother. "What is a traitor?" the boy wants to know. One who swears an oath and fails to keep it, and so must be hanged. And who hangs him? "Honest men." The son declares, "Then the liars and swearers are fools, for there are liars and swearers enow to beat the honest men and hang up them" (IV, ii, 45–58).

These words of the "poor monkey," as the mother fondly calls him, contain perhaps the most profound meaning of the tragedy of *Macbeth,* and it is not by chance that they are entrusted to the voice of innocence, for it is the innocent who judge the world for what it is: the theater of an impracticable justice and of the inevitable triumph of evil. When a messenger comes to warn them of the approaching murderers, the mother cries:

> Whither should I fly?
> I have done no harm. But I remember now
> I am in this earthly world, where to do harm
> Is often laudable, to do good sometime
> Accounted dangerous folly. Why then, alas,
> Do I put up that womanly defense,
> To say I have done no harm?
>
> [IV, ii, 73–79]

Her words, though more impassioned, confirm those of the child. When the first murderer enters, the scene becomes paradoxical. "Young fry of treachery!" the murderer insults the boy even as he stabs him, and, ironically, he is right. Be that as it may, Macduff's real treason, the betrayal of his family, will go unpunished, as his wife intuitively knows. No one will brand it as treason.

This scene (IV, ii) and the following one, which presents the dialogue-confrontation between Macduff and Malcolm, are, in my opinion, two monumentally important passages in the autobiography of the work, comparable to no other scene in the Shakespearean universe but that of Hamlet's advice to the actors. In these few pages of *Macbeth*, the entire tragic edifice is shaken and all but shattered. The blow is violent and difficult to disguise, but Shakespeare succeeds in controlling its effects. It is my intention to show why and how he does this. If we recall first certain basic historical facts concerning the tragedy of *Macbeth*, they will help us to understand what takes place on the creative level.

In the summer of 1606, King Christian of Denmark paid a royal visit to England, and Shakespeare was commissioned by King James to write a tragedy in honor of the occasion. Written in haste, *Macbeth* betrays signs of its immediate purpose. First, the play is short: the royal guests must not be wearied, and the king's distaste for lengthy dramas disregarded. Second, the theme of darkness, rich in symbolic resonances, is amply developed; a gloomy setting is more easily produced at court than would have been feasible in a daylight performance at the Globe. Furthermore, several allusions link the spectators to the action of the drama: Duncan's visit to Macbeth's castle contrasts with Christian's reception by James; the English king's forebears (beginning with Banquo, who, in Holinshed's *Chronicles* is an indefensible traitor) are all portrayed as patently honorable men.

The drama may be an apology for the good king and his right to reign and an emphatic condemnation of the usurpation of power. Duncan represents the good king; he speaks exactly as a good king ought to speak, according to the *Basilikon Doron,* a tract on the nature of royal authority written by King James. The king had earlier concerned himself with the subject of witchcraft in a work entitled *Demonology,* and it is clear that at the time he believed in the malign influence of witches. By the year

1606, he may no longer have held these beliefs, as is suggested by H. N. Paul, but he did not make his views known. We understand the significance of the witches in Macbeth—they pose the problem and incite the protagonist to action; but what was Shakespeare's purpose in giving them such prominence in a tragedy designed primarily to be performed before the king and his court?

The answer is somewhat ambiguous. It seems to me that *Macbeth* is assailed by contrasting exigencies which at times intersect with violence, and only the extraordinary poetic power, perhaps unmatched in the whole of the Shakespearean theater, unites them. Contradictions and improbabilities are dissolved by a mystical force, and it requires a cold, objective effort on the part of the reader to bring them to light. Almost every phrase is an allusion, every verse an epigraph; as the long years of a reign are reduced to a maelstrom of bloody days and sleepless nights, the kind of argumentation that characterizes Hamlet's long delay becomes in *Macbeth* the expression of a frenzy of action that consumes itself. A spasmodic haste replaces the brooding idleness. Yet no sooner do we pause to reflect, as in our opening comments on the scene at Macduff's castle, than questions arise.

Macbeth is rich in references to contemporary events. Among the most important are the thwarted Gunpowder Plot, which occurred only a few months prior to the drafting of the play; the trial of the Jesuits who supported the "Machiavellian" doctrine of equivocation; the hurricane of 1606; and the witch trials. As any thoughtful reader knows, an aesthetic appreciation of a work like *Macbeth* is not dependent on this sort of information, but the awareness of being faced with a complex system does induce a certain desire for knowledge.

The laudatory allusions to King James are, for the most part, not hard to recognize; those to the traitors who conspired in the Gunpowder Plot are no less obvious. And the elements of the play designed to gratify the royal need for adulation show that Shakespeare, as a thorough professional, did not shirk an obligatory task. Clearly, Malcolm and Duncan are brought in as proof of the legitimacy of the Scottish king's succession to the English throne, but we are left in a quandary as to the witches. The subject unquestionably held a fascination for James. Shakespeare, following Holinshed, accomplished two aims with one stroke: he satisfied the emotional needs of the sovereign while giving him an opportunity to condemn the protagonist. The fact remains, however, that James had believed in the power of witches, as evidenced by his writings, so the supernatural aspect of the play would appear to be a rather dubious medium of felicitation for his changed attitude. Or does the author wish to convey something other than this, something that comes to him only in flashes of a disquieting intuition?

This supposition is magnified when one turns to another episode: the sleep-walking scene that precedes Lady Macbeth's death (v, i). This is the climax of the prolonged obsession with insomnia that torments the protagonists. As has frequently been remarked, sleep, like food, has a fundamentally symbolic quality in *Macbeth:* to sleep and eat regularly and well is to be in harmony with nature and oneself. The banquet interrupted by the appearance of Banquo's ghost—the uneaten repast—portends a sleepless night. In the course of the play a curious exchange of roles is effected. In the beginning it is Macbeth who appears to be plagued by insomnia; after the murder of Duncan he hears a voice cry, "Sleep no more!" and later, after Banquo's murder and the appearance of his ghost, has to be led away by Lady Macbeth to seek tranquillity in repose. But the malady originally manifested in Macbeth is transmitted to his wife, and it is she who is stricken by an extreme and irremediable form of ravaged sleep. Various interpretations have been offered for this unexpected transformation in so cold and obdurate a woman. Nothing in the play has prepared us for her final breakdown, which might rather have been expected of her husband, who instead bears up and retains his lucidity even in the face of catastrophe.

The most ingenious of the explanations, advanced by Sigmund Freud among others, is of a critical-aesthetic nature, and suggests that Shakespeare strove for metaphorical rather than psychological consistency, sometimes shifting a quality from one character to another without great regard for verisimilitude. But such an explanation is hardly convincing here, and becomes even less so when one simple but well-documented fact is considered: King James himself suffered from insomnia and was very much interested in the phenomenon of somnambulism, in which he saw an element of magic that fascinated him. A knowledge of these traits clarifies the picture: once again Macbeth adumbrates a characteristic of the king, but at the point of carrying the similarity to its logical conclusion the author's discretion gains the upper hand. Let us not go too far, he seems to imply; if there must be insomnia, attribute it to Lady Macbeth rather than risk having the sovereign see himself in the protagonist. If true, this interpretation only serves to confirm the fact that Shakespeare was quite conscious of his allusions to James—allusions that could scarcely be termed benign by the reader, the cloak of ambiguous adulation notwithstanding.

All this would be of only relative importance were it not for the fact that it throws a new light on the intentions, and still more on the significance, of the tragedy. In this context it is useful to recall the climate in which the works belonging to the "great period"—from *Hamlet* to *Timon of Athens*—were born. According to Theodore Spencer, *Hamlet* represents a decisive development as far as the representation of human nature is concerned: the harmonious vision that had inspired the previous works is fractured, and there unfolds an irrevocable conflict that is rooted in the universe itself. In the progression to a more mature phase, *Hamlet* occupies a place of paramount importance, and I should like to add a few considerations to those already advanced by the many perceptive interpreters of this major drama.

Hamlet is the first Shakespearean tragic hero to doubt the legitimacy of his own role. His destiny is that of *witnessing.* Having witnessed his father's glorious reign, he is then witness to the corrupt rule of the fratricidal Claudius when he assumes the royal prerogatives. In the atmosphere of regal pomp, Hamlet affects the disquieting posture of the *fool*, without ceasing to be the court intellectual, poet, and subtle rhetorician, whose imaginative faculty surpasses that of his philosopher friend Horatio. Hamlet alone talks with his father's ghost; he alone is in contact with a world whose truths are revealed in hallucinations and lightning flashes, a world of unconscious certitudes prefigured in the form and raiment of the murdered king. Hamlet is the court artist. And the other artists are the itinerant players he will use to unmask Claudius. It is Hamlet's destiny to be present at the collapse of one dynasty and the beginning of a new order which he dimly senses is to be perfidious, and in order to expose it as such he needs *proof.* His reproaches to his mother are addressed to the very concept of the royal crown: Are you a whore, then, giving yourself to everyone, being passed from hand to hand?

Is it worth recalling that at the time of the writing of the great tragedies power was being transferred from the Tudors to the Stuarts, from Elizabeth to James. The fascination exercised upon her subjects by Elizabeth need not be emphasized. One has only to remark that the flourishing of the theater during that period would not have been possible without the sense of stability, security, and absolute legitimacy that her long reign had communicated to her subjects, to noblemen and artists alike. It cannot be mere chance that immediately after her death (and even immediately before, as can be seen in certain intimations in *Hamlet* and *Julius Caesar*), Shakespeare's work reflects a kind of inner agitation. By means of theatrical schemes already tested, his poetic force ends in endowing the problems that afflicted England during those years with a cosmic density. The unaccustomed insecurity, the sense of being present at the end of a halcyon era, the cumulative foreboding rumbling through a kingdom that felt itself divested of genuine protection—all these are deeply etched in the pages of *Hamlet, Macbeth,* and *King Lear,* the great dramas of power overthrown. Nature too becomes the stage of a universal drama. An apocalyptic air, as of the imminent end of the world, must have had political as well as personal motivations. *Timon of Athens* marks the point of perhaps the greatest pessimism in the entire Shakespeare oeuvre; the nature of power emerges in all its horror.

By the year 1606, the immediate repercussions to the succession lie in the past. The general discontent, however, has deepened, and with it a sense of having entered upon a period of irreparable decadence (one need only think of the evolution of a man like John Donne toward an increasingly desolate vision of life). In Shakespeare, too, beginning with *Hamlet,* one notes a pervasive climate of nostalgia: the land is now "a sterile promontory," the kingdom "an unweeded garden." Court festivals have deteriorated to drunken revels, and ceremonial to mere sham. The wisdom of Polonius is banal pedantry; Claudius and the Queen are an imitation of a happily married couple; and Laertes is an impersonation of spirited, valorous youth. In Hamlet's compulsion to unmask the lie, Ophelia, incapable of pretense, is reduced by him to genuine madness. From this point on, in Shakespeare's tragedies madness becomes the destiny of those who, like Ophelia and Lear, see things for what they are. Even Hamlet requires a fiction to "catch the conscience of the King," and at the close of the tragedy, begs Horatio to "draw thy breath in pain, / To tell my story."

It is Horatio who takes the situation in hand when Fortinbras arrives; Horatio announces that he will recount "How these things came about." The tragedy of Hamlet seems about to begin again: "call the noblest to the audience," cries Fortinbras; "Bear Hamlet, like a soldier, to the stage." The *audience* includes the spectators as well, and the *stage* is also that of the theater. Among so many fictions, at least art survives.

But of what will this story speak?

> Of carnal, bloody and unnatural acts,
> Of accidental judgments, casual slaughters,
> Of deaths put on by cunning and forc'd cause,

And, in this upshot, purposes mistook
Fall'n on th' inventors' heads.

[v, ii, 384–388]

We are now in the realm of the "poor player" later hypothesized by Macbeth; we are in the poetics proclaimed by the witches in the opening scene of *Macbeth:* "Fair is foul and foul is fair." Through his perception of the incomprehensible tragedy of life, Hamlet is the first of Shakespeare's characters to challenge tragedy as a literary genre nourished by classical moral and intellectual lucidity. There begins a chapter of Shakespeare's work that reflects hopeless confusion and that will reach its climax in that "comedy of the grotesque" which will be *King Lear*. What G. Wilson Knight says of *King Lear* can be generalized to apply to *Hamlet, Macbeth,* and *Othello* as well: "The tragedy is most poignant in that it is purposeless, unreasonable. . . . It faces the very absence of tragic purpose." (*The Wheel of Fire*, pp. 174–175).

When Shakespeare goes to the royal court to present *Macbeth*, he finds himself in a situation not unlike that of Hamlet in the third act: now Shakespeare's will be the play "to catch the conscience of the King." But Shakespeare will have to be even more adroit than Hamlet; there must be no mistake; one false step will mean his ruin. Once again, necessity proves to be the mother of invention—even of genius. *Macbeth* emerges as a masterpiece of contradictory meanings unified by a violence that leaves the spectator no time to catch his breath. The expedients contrived to gratify the sovereign are undeniably obvious yet at the same time subtly venomous. Let us take the murdered King Duncan as one example. If he is meant to represent the "good king" (conforming to James's *Basilikon Doron*), his brief appearances, sketched in somewhat idyllic tints, seem almost a travesty in the atmosphere of the drama's violence. Rather than good, Duncan seems merely inept, not even a warrior king, since his battles are all won for him by others.

There is also the whole question of the legitimacy of power.

135

Banquo emerges as somewhat better than his prototype in Holinshed, and it is quite clear why: he is the founder of the house that has put James on the throne. But quite apart from the fact that this Scottish king cannot possibly represent a legitimate English king to Shakespeare's contemporaries, there remains the fundamental question: How is this legitimacy to be proved? For instance, do those who rebel against Macbeth after he becomes king transgress the laws of loyalty? It is no easy matter to determine where treason begins and ends. Whereas Hamlet is haunted by a nightmare of legitimacy violated, Macbeth is animated by an unbridled will to violate a recognized hereditary right. If both are guided by specters and visions, it is because their reasoning is lost in a labyrinth of hypotheses. The will to act that animated both heroes is transmuted into ghosts and a chorus of witches that voice the precepts of the dramas.

This grotesque objectification is crucial. It seems clear to Hamlet that the principles of tragedy are rooted in the irrational, and this is why he, the sophistic intellectual and lover of hair-splitting wordplay, equivocates throughout the entire development of the work. Indeed, he has no great desire to enter into a drama as inconclusive as that enjoined by a ghost avid for revenge. This Hamlet who, through Shakespeare, had read Montaigne and can always find a reason for deferring the act of vengeance, only resolves to act after realizing that he is caught in a trap and may die before he has consummated what he wishes.

Macbeth also finds himself constrained to enter into a hopeless drama. The difference is that whereas any lack of logic is contrary to Hamlet's discriminating sensibility, the distraction and chaos of Macbeth's tragedy are largely of his own making. The famous monologue after Lady Macbeth's death is the quintessence of the play's central theme: once good and evil, fair and foul, have been conjoined, the direction of the action consigned to the witches, and Macbeth made the royal protagonist, what can be expected if not a chaotic, clamorous spectacle? It is this that Shakespeare presents to his audience: a drama "signifying nothing," in which all in turn lament its absurdity. "Confusion now hath made his masterpiece," says Macduff, on discovering Duncan's murder. And it is not only a question of moral chaos, of an ethical harmony destroyed, but of an aesthetic principle violated. We are immersed in the brew conjured by the witches according to their infernal recipe in Act IV. This too is an *ars poetica,* a jumble of everything thrown together in a weird, repellent mixture in which nothing relates to anything else.

The two protagonists of *Macbeth* anxiously set about trying to activate their drama from the outset. In vain does Lady Macbeth give her husband a lesson in dissimulation; in vain does she prescribe the very expression of his face. Macbeth is fated to betray himself, for, having entered upon the drama of life as actor-king, he wants to live it with passion, and therein lie the seeds of his failure. He stumbles onto the stage like a clown, assuming "borrowed robes," "a fruitless crown," "a barren sceptre." The dialogue between the husband and wife while they prepare to execute their crime has the timbre of actors about to make an entrance on the stage. The wife even speaks of changing her sex—an oblique allusion to women's roles being played by boys in the Elizabethean theater.

The metaphor of the actor, which runs through all of Shakespeare's work, finds in the king (or aspiring king) its most apt and cogent use, for there was a general acceptance of the analogy between the two vocations. Macbeth's maladroit haste in donning the royal robes is a symptom of his unfitness to interpret the role of the protagonist. Like a second-rate actor, he is incapable of emerging from his assigned role (an insight that will also be found in Diderot's *Paradoxe du comédien*). Once embarked upon his bloody course, he cannot stop himself; the action of interpreting (to act means both to take action and to play) possesses him, giving him no respite. He commits murder almost blindly; he is the actor who cannot relinquish his persona. When, during her raving, Lady Macbeth tries to wipe out the blood spot on her hand, it is as if it were some sort of stage makeup resistant to removal; what had once been action and memory now becomes passion and remorse.

Furthermore, the time is "out of joint," for everything happens at the wrong time in the famous drama "signifying nothing": cues are picked up too early or too late; the actors' timing is off. In Lady Macbeth's words:

> Thy letters have transported me beyond
> This ignorant present, and I feel now
> The future in the instant.
>
> [I, v, 56–58]

And Macbeth himself, before the murder of Duncan, says:

> If it were done, when 'tis done, then 'twere well
> It were done quickly. If th' assassination
> Could trammel up the consequence, and catch
> With his surcease, success: that but this blow
> Might be the be-all and the end-all—here,
> But here, upon this bank and shoal of time,
> We'd jump the life to come.
>
> [I, vii, 1–7]

These lines show the two protagonists' chimerical sense of time, immured as they are in a visionary notion of its essence. In fact they are in search of absolute time, which can be attained only through hallucination, through a leap into a present beyond the future. The actual present coincides with the imbalance of the reeling action: when Macbeth asks, "What is the night?" his wife replies, "Almost at odds with the morning, which is which" (III, iv, 126–127). And when the present is past it becomes irreparable; it is neither rectified nor made acceptable. The action becomes part of the past, but not of incontrovertible time. In the monologue after his wife's death, Macbeth describes life as divided into *yesterdays* and *tomorrows,* which transform the recurrent present into a chaos, "full of sound and fury." This realization produces another visionary leap beyond the future: if his wife had died *hereafter,* "There would have been a time for such a word." This *time* can be nothing less than unattainable time, beyond choice, beyond remorse. The mechanism of haste, in which this perception is expressed, is that of the guilty conscience.

Through reflection on the problem of power, nature itself is brought into question. Macbeth's speech to the murderers who are to kill Banquo is the focal point of this reinterpretation of man.

> FIRST MURTHERER: We are men, my liege.
> MACBETH:
>> Ay, in the catalogue ye go for men,
>> As hounds and greyhounds, mongrels, spaniels, curs,
>> Shoughs, waterrugs and demi-wolves, are clipt
>> All by the name of dogs. The valued file
>> Distinguishes the swift, the slow, the subtle,
>> The housekeeper, the hunter, every one
>> According to the gift which bounteous nature
>> Hath in him clos'd, whereby he does receive
>> Particular addition, from the bill
>> That writes them all alike; and so of men.
>>
>> [III, i, 92–102]

This nomenclature of distinguishing qualities within a species bears a striking resemblance to a passage in Niccolò Machiavelli's *The Prince* (Modern Library College Edition [New York: Random House, 1950] pp. 56–57).

> I state that all men, and especially princes, who are placed at a greater height, are reputed for certain qualities which bring them either praise or blame. Thus one is considered liberal, another *misero* or miserly ... ; one a free giver, another rapacious; one cruel, another merciful; one a breaker of his word, another trustworthy; one effeminate and pusillanimous, another fierce and high-spirited; one humane, another haughty; one lascivious, another chaste;

one frank, another astute; one hard, another easy; one serious, another frivolous; one religious, another an unbeliever, and so on.

The philosophical kernel of both the above passages lies in the notion of man as an empty vessel that must be filled with qualifying attributes—attributes which all relate to an *action*. Man is nothing until he acts; indeed, only action renders definition possible. Action is the vital manifestation that defines a man while at the same time imprisoning him in a role, which may engender a metaphysical anxiety, as in the case of Hamlet, for whom the great enterprises he dreams of "lose the name of action." Machiavelli's prince too is defined through his action, which is at the same time *being* and *seeming,* taking action and playing a role; which shows that *Macbeth* is deeply indebted to the Machiavellian philosophy of power.

Looking back, we can see in Shakespeare's plays the nature of the progression in this conception of power. The description of the kingdom as a well-cultivated garden, which is found in *Richard II,* represents a stage of optimism at which political harmony is adduced as a possible "imitation" of natural harmony; therefore the apologue is related as truth and accepted as such by the writer and the character. But this is certainly not true of the crisis in *Hamlet.* Ulysses' famous speech in *Troilus and Cressida"* (I, iii, 75ff.), frequently cited by critics as exemplifying Shakespeare's creed, is raddled with falseness and deceit; and it is not without reason that the author assigns it to Ulysses, the proverbial liar. The sun king at the center of the universe, a Ptolemaic vision, cannot appear to be simply naïve in Shakespeare's eyes. At the moment, the harmony and legitimacy of power are defensible only through the medium of the *well-spoken lie,* through a persuasive rhetoric that is inspired by the desecration of the farcical Trojan War, in which it seems strange that the only serious element should be Ulysses' discourse. The great tragedies take another forward step: power is viewed as *substantial illegitimacy* that is self-perpetuating, and as *apparent legitimacy* that is redeemed by success and guaranteed by the form in which it is presented to the world. When Lady Macbeth says to her husband, "look like the innocent flower, / But be the serpent underneath 't," she is trying to give him a lesson both in acting and in imitating nature, as if nature were to act its own innocence. Here the evil within man seems to reproduce the evil of reality outside him. Falsity is *natural,* and to be a traitor is most normal.

The predicament of Macbeth and his wife is that, in contradistinction to the serpent, they are crushed by their guilt. They have "bad dreams," as Hamlet would say, and these will bring them to their ruin. In fact they are not playing the roles of goodness at all, but rather those of evil. They feel from the outset that they are doing something profoundly unnatural, and even to themselves become images of nature outraged. Macbeth concludes his final speech in Act I with the words: "False face must hide what the false heart doth know." Take note of this "false heart"; it is the weak link, the infirm pillar of the argument. A true Machiavellian might feel that he had a false face, but never a false heart; the heart is what it is. If both are felt to be false, a contradiction arises, and one enters the realm of bad acting—that is, of evil that aims at being discovered. The entire second act of *Macbeth* is an illustration of this destiny of failure. The success of the criminal enterprise is only an apparent success. In the scene that follows the assassination of Duncan (II, ii), Macbeth and his wife are already assailed by so much remorse that they court punishment and damnation. Suspicion immediately falls upon them: Malcolm and Donalbain, after clearly hinting at treason, depart in haste, as do Macduff and Ross in the following scene. In that scene an old man appears and closes the act with words of proverbial wisdom:

> God's benison go with you, and with those
> That would make good of bad and friends of foes!
>
> [II, iv, 40-41]

"Make good of bad" is a highly ambiguous phrase. It can mean the actual transformation of evil into good, which would conform with the traditional interpretation of *Macbeth* as a tragedy of the formidable struggle between the forces of good and evil (the former "natural" and the latter "unnatural"). But it can also mean "Blessed are those who make good of evil, making it appear so by altering its face"—a new Machiavellian precept addressed to a Macduff who later will evoke the damning epithet of traitor from Lady Macduff.

Meanwhile Macbeth, impetuously and for no apparent reason, has Banquo murdered. He then falls prey to hallucinations; when, at the banquet, his victim's ghost appears, his reaction betrays his guilt, and everyone realizes that it was he who perpetrated the crime—a realization he subconsciously desires. Devastated by remorse, the husband and wife rush headlong to their ruin. They now resemble the serpent, though without the flower, and all their efforts to imitate nature notwithstanding, their actions end in becoming *disimitation*. To *disimitate* nature is to commit evil in such a way as to direct it against oneself. By the middle of the third act, Macbeth's days are numbered:

> Better be with the dead,
> Whom we, to gain our peace, have sent to peace,
> Than on the torture of the mind to lie
> In restless ecstasy.

> [III, ii, 19-22]

Machiavelli taught that the *virtù* of the leader is judged by the effect of his action: if he loses his kingdom, he becomes a negative person, and all his sins will be revealed, as on Judgment Day. But the reverse is equally true: if he becomes a person who is manifestly negative, he inevitably loses his kingdom. In *Richard III*, an earlier tragedy in which there prevails an essentially anti-Machiavellian climate of conflict between the forces of good and evil, it is precisely the villain, who displays his acting ability. Vaunting his Machiavellianism, Richard will be routed by those forces he is incapable of counterfeiting: goodness triumphs over evil as truth over a lie, for in contrast to vice, goodness cannot disguise itself. Even when skillfully wielded, the power of the wicked endures only for the length of the performance; its life span is ineluctably limited. In *Hamlet,* however, it is the good character who must simulate in order to rend the fiction of the evildoers, those who perform well but not well enough to last to the end—an intuition that is halfway between the insights of *Richard III* and those of *Macbeth.* In the last play the villain has become a synonym, not for the actor, but for the bad actor. What happens to the positive characters in *Macbeth*? Are they like Richard's vanquishers? Or do they in turn go through a metamorphosis? For if the conflict between and actor and his opposite is one between fiction and truth, the contrast between a bad actor and his opposite must manifest itself as the difference between a bad performance and a good one. We are then in a world composed entirely of actors, and if Macbeth is imperfect, who are those who manage with the skill of the accomplished actor?

Let us first consider Duncan. He does not appear to be taking part in a tragedy. Arriving at Macbeth's castle, he perceives it in an idyllic landscape (Banquo's observations on the delicate air and singing birds furnish an ironic commentary on Duncan's simplicity). The king is gentle and trusting, and it is his fate to let himself be killed. If the theme of the play were the stuggle between good and evil, it would end at this point with the categorical victory of evil.

But now let us consider Malcolm, Duncan's son and claimant to the throne, and Macduff, a Scottish nobleman. In the roster of the drama's characters, these two are arrayed on the side of the just; when they meet (IV, iii), their animosity toward Macbeth is expressed in terms of harsh moral judgment. This scene immediately follows the massacre at Macduff's castle, and though the news has not yet reached them, it is in the air. Their dialogue is, in the main, taken from Holinshed, with Shakespeare adding certain allusive and strikingly ambiguous lines of his own. Not sure that he can trust Macduff, Malcolm repeatedly provokes him, and their exchanges become a skirmish in which the most dissimulated blows are the most decisive. Macduff's decision to flee, though he knows Macbeth's character and leaves his family defenseless, lacks all justification and can only be interpreted as either thoroughly unconscionable or deliberately criminal. I tend to accept the latter hypothesis, believing that the author himself had arrived at this conclusion in the course of writing the play.

Let us reconstruct this process of the play's composition: in the feverish haste with which Shakespeare composed the text—submerged as he was in the singular climate of the times and because of the personal and ideological crisis caused by his complex, contradictory feelings about the man who had commissioned the play—he followed Holinshed's plot for the first three acts, providing it with a fantastic and metaphorical form. The positive and negative characters were already prescribed, and there was no reason to alter their roles except for precautionary considerations about James, and then only in part. Meanwhile the play had acquired vertiginous contradictions in all of the established roles and a unique psychological penetration in the exploration of the nature of evil. When Malcolm and Macduff reappeared upon the scene in Act IV, it was difficult to present them as two new incarnations of "the power of good," in the manner of Duncan, because Shakespeare now knew that this form of goodness is destined to fail, and knew too that the type of problem created by Macbeth's actions cannot be resolved by an antinomian counterpoising of black and white, chaos and rectitude, treason and legitimacy.

At this point Shakespeare must have been somewhat surprised by the *Chronicle's* description of the massacre at the castle, which furnished him with the only possible pretext for a reinterpretation of the character of Macduff. Shakespeare has made of this brief scene the center of an adamant problem which restates the question of life from the side of the good—that is, of the inevitable victims. This is done without parody, for Lady Macduff and her child are not trying to preserve any sort of power. They are genuinely and irrevocably betrayed, as Cordelia will be in *King Lear;* they are the truly good, the pure in heart spoken of in the Gospels, the foolish ones with neither hope nor reward in this world. As the child senses, an "honest" power cannot exist, and it is precisely the contradiction between honesty and power that the meeting of Malcolm and Macduff will help resolve.

Malcolm's first allusion to the question is in the following lines:

> This tyrant, whose sole name blisters our tongues,
> Was once thought honest; you have lov'd him well;
> He hath not touch'd you yet. I am young; but something
> You may discern of him through me.
>
> [IV, iii, 12-15]

Thus the Waith edition, (The Yale Shakespeare) which follows the 1623 folio; but the majority of modern editors of *Macbeth* have substituted the word "deserve" for "discern" (among others, Kenneth Muir in the Arden *Macbeth* and J. Dover Wilson in the Cambridge edition). Even those who like Waith's rendition have been faithful to the folio, have entered into tortuous explanations of this passage, unable to accept the simplest implication of its meaning, which is: But you can see (recognize) in me (Malcolm) something of him (Macbeth). And if Macduff sees in Malcolm something he has in common with Macbeth, he will try to win his protection in the same way he would Macbeth's.

The text continues:

> and wisdom
> To offer up a weak, poor, innocent lamb
> T' appease an angry god.
>
> [IV, iii, 15-17]

In the light of the previous semantic construction, the traditional interpretation of this passage too needs revision. What Malcolm implies is: You have long been in the service of Macbeth; now join me. But where is your credibility? Thus far, we know, he has not touched you, but what guarantee can you give me of your new fidelity—*the lives of your dear ones perhaps?* However involuted and ambiguous his expression, this, it seems to me, is his meaning. If the words "innocent lamb" refer to Macduff's family, then the "angry god" to be appeased is not Macbeth but rather Malcolm, who makes a show of defending himself while in fact attacking. Macduff grasps his meaning at once and retorts, "I am not treacherous" (l. 18). Malcolm now broadens the attack: That may well be true, but Macbeth is, and it is possible that you have been subjected to his malign influence; though you have a good and virtuous look, the brightest angels can come to ruin through sin. In short, I may conceivably trust you on the strength of your appearance. Malcolm is temporizing, inviting Macduff to reveal himself more fully but his interlocutor is a match for him. I have lost all hope, Macduff exclaims, taking refuge in a phrase that is intentionally vague. For Macduff is not in haste; he knows that soon there will be conclusive evidence of the hostility between him and Macbeth, and he will have no further need for words. Malcolm persists, however, seeking to anticipate him:

> Perchance even there where I did find my doubts.
> Why in that rawness left you wife and child,
> Those precious motives, those strong knots of love,
> Without leave-taking? I pray you,
> Let not my jealousies be your dishonors,
> But mine own safeties. You may be rightly just,
> Whatever I shall think.
>
> [IV, iii, 25–31]

This is a direct enough hit: Now you see that I know quite well what is going on—which still does not mean that I blame you. It all depends on what you have in mind. In his reply, Macduff guards against giving his reason for leaving his family unprotected, and instead, launches into a rhetorical apostrophe on the misfortunes of his country, after which he feigns a desire to leave: "I would not be the villain that thou think'st." Which means, again translated into explicit terms: If you have grasped my meaning, I'll not let you say so openly. Detain me if you wish.

And Malcolm detains him ("Be not offended") with a fresh and unexpected reversal. At this point in their confrontation a significant development is apparent: each knows that the other is aware of his performance. To refrain from committing an error in the presentation means to affirm the measure of one's stature, to be accepted for something beyond the words that are no more than the actor's disguise.

The power of this dialogue lies in its covert meaning; the two men are like chess players bent on settling a score, executing a series of brilliant tactical variations with false attacks and defensive retreats. The height of this exercise in skill is reached in Malcolm's famous profession of villainy. The episode is found in Holinshed, but Shakespeare, with unfailing mastery, places it before the disclosure of the massacre. Why do you wish me to be king? asks Malcolm. I am inordinately lustful; all your wives and daughters would not be enough to gratify my appetite. We can see to that, replies Macduff, still waiting to find out what he is driving at. I am excessively avaricious, continues Malcolm; I will possess myself of all your properties. A pernicious vice, responds Macduff, yet Scotland can satisfy it if you become king. After all, you have other merits. None, declares Malcolm; I am a sink of iniquity, a dunghill of depravity; nothing speaks in my favor. Then Macduff appears to abandon hope, delivers an eloquent monologue, and is on the point of parting from him for good when Malcolm confesses to having lied in order to test him.

When Holinshed's version of this episode is compared to Shakespeare's, several points of similarity are evident, but there is one decisive difference which seems not to have been remarked before. Holinshed's record of the dialogue gives credence to Macduff's good faith; both his alarm and his disillusionment are portrayed as sincere. In Shakespeare's play, however, they seem to me to be presented in a very different light. Here Malcolm is not trying to provoke Macduff's indignation, but to ascertain the degree to which he is capable of simulating indignation at a given moment. In short, he is testing him again, not as an upright man, but as an actor. Their dialogue, in a disguised form, echoes that between Richard and Buckingham in *Richard III*.

RICHARD:

> Come, cousin, canst thou quake, and change thy colour,
> Murther thy breath in middle of a word,
> And then again begin, and stop again,
> As if thou wert distraught and mad with terror?

BUCKINGHAM:

> Tut! I can counterfeit the deep tragedian,
> Speak and look back, and pry on every side,
> Tremble and start at wagging of a straw,
> Intending deep suspicion: ghastly looks
> Are at my service, like enforced smiles.

[III, v, 1–9]

Here Richard is the stronger and asks for a concrete demonstration of his ally's performing ability. The relation between the two characters has, in this instance, been explicitly defined, and the audience is not left in doubt. They are villains and must be revealed as such, whereas Malcolm and Macduff must continue to play their roles and can be understood only through the veil of words. Moreover, the audience—particularly that royal audience to which the author originally addressed the tragedy of *Macbeth*—must be reassured, and only one who so desires can penetrate the truth.

The essence of Malcolm's inquiry is: What will you do if I simulate such a monstrous character? And Macduff replies: For my part, I'll portray indignation. Malcolm is sufficiently satisfied with his response to launch into a monologue on his own virtues, which for the most part are of Shakespeare's devising. It is this speech that, in my opinion, offers conclusive proof of the author's transformation of the scene. In Holinshed, Malcolm is

restricted to saying: "Be of good comfort Makduffe, for I haue
none of these vices before remembered, but haue iested with
thee in this manner, onelie to prooue thy mind."

But Shakespeare's Malcolm says a good deal more:

> I am yet
> Unknown to woman, never was forsworn,
> Scarcely have coveted what was mine own,
> At no time broke my faith, would not betray
> The devil to his fellow, and delight
> No less in truth than life. My first false speaking
> Was this upon myself.
>
> [IV, iii, 125–131]

A similar and equally extravagant self-portrait, with many
points in common but with opposite intent, is that of Boccaccio's Ceppelletto (*Decameron*,I,1), the first *ante-litteram* Machiavellian figure of the Italian tradition and one unquestionably representative of diabolical dissimulation. The catalogue of virtues
turns out to be no less incredible than that of vices. Needing to
find a definition of himself, the future monarch resorts to the
idealization of the prince sanctioned by a secular literature. It
is the portrait of a new Duncan. But Malcolm is not Duncan
and knows the difference—a distinction absolutely clear to
Machiavelli—between being good and seeming to be good; the
distinction is decisive when a kingdom is at stake. In short, the
meeting between Malcolm and Macduff represents the passage
from black to white magic, from diabolic witchcraft to holy
sorcery. Even the episode of the king as healer (a bow to James)
can be viewed in this perspective. He embodies qualities of
power and of ambition masked by saintliness which were seen in
Malcolm and Macduff. This is in direct contrast to the witches,
who expose the weakness of Macbeth, the criminal who appears
to be exactly what he is.

The shedding of Machiavellian light over the entire play cannot help but alter its meaning. The antiprince polemic in *Richard*

III indicated a remarkable faith in the possibility of separating the worlds of darkness and light, the heaven of virtue and the realm of fallen angels. Gloucester, the future king, who has already proclaimed himself a disciple of Machiavelli in *Henry VI, Part III*, proceeds to show himself for what he is in the opening monologue of *Richard III*, thus establishing the premises of his inevitable downfall. His personality exudes evil, as is instantly apparent in the symbolic deformation of his body, which causes dogs to bark at him as he limps by, as though they have caught the scent of sulphur. The frenetic crescendo of his actions transforms him into a monstrous bloodstained puppet. Clearly, he *wants* to reveal himself; the sanctimonious mien that has won popular sympathy is so obvious to the audience that it will become apparent sooner or later to his enemies. His defeat is proof of how a professed Machiavellianism fails to work. Evil, like a started beast, is brought to bay. The *villain* never ceases to be the *villain:* this is his theatrical destiny; hence in *Richard III* the struggle is still between the just and the unjust, the legitimate and the illegitimate. Richard and Buckingham are not only evil; they are the buffoons of evil. There is a kind of cheerful professionalism about their performances, at the conclusion of which they seem to execute a graceful pirouette and exit into the darkness, there to reside among the other puppets of evil.

Hamlet has brought to a crux a similar situation by opposing a world falsely shaped to the measure of harmonious and legitimate men: the court of Claudius, which conceals the infamy of a Richard. Yet *Hamlet* preserves a trace of the ancient optimism: evil is finally exposed, even at the cost of bringing the good to their ruin. Claudius' mise en scène cannot withstand the blows dealt it by Hamlet's mise en scène, and in the revelation of this truth is inscribed the destiny that awaits the usurper. A king who proclaims his Machiavellianism (Richard) paves the way for his own downfall; a king whose Machiavellianism is exposed by others (Claudius) is on the brink of downfall. But a king who is genuinely Machiavellian—what is his image, his fate?

In the first place, his nature should not be perceptible either to the audience or to the other characters in the drama. The spectators and the actors form a system of communication within the theatrical experience: what is known to one group will be revealed to the other. An awareness by some of the characters cannot be withheld from the others except for a period of time in the course of the play's action. When Richard's wickedness is conveyed to the audience, it is only a matter of time before it is revealed to the characters in the play. As the protagonist of evil, Macbeth follows this same trajectory: the audience witnesses the evolution of his iniquity and confidently waits for its unmasking; were this not so, the tragedy would become a glorification of royal criminality, which is not Shakespeare's intention. With great circumspection and ambiguity, he ventures to represent, not the conflict between the forces of good and evil, but the conflict between *evil well performed* and *evil poorly peformed.* If Macbeth and his wife, the two characters representing evil, succeed in achieving their goal, their victory will be total, and the audience too will be caught in the trap of verisimilitude.

The true Machiavellian prince is not one who seems to have read the treatise of that name, but one who, if anything, will write the anti-Machiavellian work, one to whom the Florentine's pages do not seem to apply, for a true Machiavellian prince must always appear to be good. Therefore Macbeth and Lady Macbeth fail in performance on the battlefield of power. The genuine leader is distinguished by a want of feeling for the afflictions of mankind. Remorse, not guilt, is the undoing of this homicidal couple; it is passion that renders them clumsy and fanciful, quick to succumb as soon as they are confronted by an effective foe. Let us examine the double prediction of the witches (this too has its origin in Holinshed) that harm can come to Macbeth from "none of woman born," and that he will meet defeat only when the surrounding wood shall come to Dunsinane. The second prophecy is, above all, a spectacular device: Malcolm's army, screened by leafy boughs, advancing on Dunsinane is a splendid *coup de théâtre,* a translation into images of a truth that has risen to the surface of Shakespeare's consciousness

—to wit, that Macbeth's enemies will defeat him on the plane of simulation and disguise. As for "none of woman born," Macbeth takes the witches' augury as a guarantee of his invincibility, since there can be no such man. Apart from the literal explanation (before killing him, Macduff will disclose to Macbeth that he "was from his mother's womb untimely ripp'd"), the phrase means that only he who is able to defeat Macbeth *on the plane of his inhumanity* will be able to defeat him politically and militarily.

Does Macduff conform to this qualification? This is the question that Malcolm has been trying to solve by means of his verbal maneuvers with Macduff. Malcolm does not attempt to elicit a confession, which would be of no use to him in any case, but rather to understand his future lieutenant. Finally, the two men reach an understanding without having compromised themselves. At this point, following a brief laudatory reference to Edward the Confessor, Ross—he who was in such haste to take his leave of Lady Macduff—arrives on the scene. Coming from Scotland, he first gives them news of the state of the kingdom; but here again the real dialogue lies beneath the surface. Ross has been informed of the massacre of Macduff's family and has come to report it; finding Macduff in conclave with Malcolm, and ignorant as to whether or not they have reached an accord, he delays his announcement. His conduct, even before the murder of Lady Macduff, makes it clear that he is cognizant of Macduff's intentions. The first question put to him by Macduff —"Stands Scotland where it did? (IV, iii, 164)—it is strange, to say the least, inasmuch as he himself has just left that country. Is he perhaps asking something of a more specific nature? Ross dares not reply, deterred by the presence of Malcolm, who asks, "What's the newest grief?" to which he gives a vague and circumspect reply: "Each minute teems a new one." Whereupon Macduff intervenes and speaks plainly:

MACDUFF: How does my wife?
ROSS: Why, well.

MACDUFF: And all my children?
ROSS: Well too.

[IV, iii, 176–177]

These four lines of dialogue are rather extraordinary, however they are understood. According to the common interpretation, Ross has come in a state of extreme anguish at having to
report the horrifying tragedy. If this were true, a more cruel and
unfeeling response would be hard to imagine. To say to Macduff
that all is well with his family, then to tell him a few minutes later
that they have been murdered, can hardly be construed as a sign
of friendship. Moreover, Ross gives no evidence of being overcome by confusion; having just made a fine speech reverberat-
ing with elaborate imagery on the state of Scotland, he now does
no more than repeat the one word "well," sounding more like a
dispassionate messenger than an anguished friend. In short, it
seems to me quite evident that the two cousins are endeavoring
to convey certain information to each other and are hindered
from doing so by the presence of Malcolm—to say nothing of the
presence of the principal spectator, a Scottish king only recently
crowned king of England, and an audience that has come to
witness the cathartic rite of evil punished and virtue rewarded.
How would such an audience react were Ross to announce that
the cousins' scheme had succeeded, that Lady Macduff and her
children were dead, and that nothing stood in the way of Macduff's being appointed Malcolm's lieutenant and the murderer
of Macbeth? In the light of certain analogies, the scene becomes
less ambiguous. Ross's reply chillingly echoes an earlier moment
in the play when Macbeth asks of Banquo's murderer (III, iv,
26–27), "But Banquo's safe?" and elicits a similar if more explicit
and heinously ironic answer: "Ay, my good lord: safe in a ditch
he bides."

Macduff perseveres: "The tyrant has not battered at their
peace?" So he expected it. Why then did he do nothing to pre-
vent the crime? This is Lady Macduff's question and Malcolm's

too, though phrased more circumspectly. Ross adroitly extricates himself by playing on the double meaning of the words "at peace": "they were well at peace when I did leave 'em." Macduff cuts short this circuitous method of communication and brusquely demands: "Be not niggard of your speech: how goes 't?" Before replying, Ross seeks Malcolm's intervention in the conversation by announcing that conditions in Scotland are such that the country is ripe for revolt against Macbeth, and Malcolm instantly concurs. Now that the situation is clear and the two men of one mind, Ross no longer hesitates to reveal what everyone already knows. There ensues a dolorous recital by Macduff with the appropriate rhetorical exhortations to revenge. Enunciated by true professionals, it is concise, decorous, and assured. One rather revealing allusion appears in Macduff's speech concerning the staging of the enterprise:

> O, I could play the woman with mine eyes,
> And braggart with my tongue.
>
> [IV, iii, 230–232]

This has already been done, however, and now it is time to act, time for the final catastrophe. When Macbeth has at last been dispatched, Malcolm proclaims his plan of action, concluding with the words: "We will perform in measure, time, and place." He has referred to the Aristotelian principles of tragedy—even using the word "perform." Here is the actor-king triumphantly reinstated after the poor performance of Macbeth, which he himself acknowledged in the words: "Life's but a walking shadow, a poor player...." The great performance of sovereignty reaffirms its right; yet the problem remains: Is this choreography only meant to deceive the ingenuous?

If our reading of the dialogue between Malcolm and Macduff is given credence, their restoration to legitimacy is the restoration of a "correct" imitation of natural processes in which an apparent order cloaks the chaos of violence; according to the vision Shakespeare is evolving, "the serpent" is under "the inno-

cent flower." Macbeth had succeeded in imitating only the serpent, not nature's conjunction of the two; in imitating evil, he
disimitated nature, arriving at an incomplete and vulnerable
evil, like a serpent coming out into the open and making itself
vulnerable. Let us recall the series of betrayals in the play. First
there is the betrayal by the thane of Cawdor—a betrayal known
to all and punished at the outset of the drama; this is followed by
Macbeth's betrayal, immediately made known to the audience,
then gradually to the other characters, and destined (theatrically
destined) to be punished; finally there is Macduff's betrayal,
known only to the victims and to those directly or indirectly
implicated in the crime. And if the betrayal is not clearly revealed to the audience, it will go unpunished.

Here we see why Shakespeare gives only hints and clues to
Macduff's behavior: the mysterious words muttered by an old
man, Lady Macduff's sudden realization of the truth, the confrontation of Macduff and Malcolm. I also believe that another
advance signal has been posted: the Porter's scene (II, iii). Critics
have recognized the historical references in his monologue and
the symbolic dimension of the character: doorkeeper of Macbeth's castle is equivalent to doorkeeper of hell. If this is true,
whoever is knocking at the gates at that moment is probably a
damned soul. The words "Remember the porter" at the end of
the monologue would seem to be an exhortation to remember
the symbolism of the scene—that men are knocking at the gate
of hell, where Beelzebub awaits them. And who is knocking?
None other than Macduff, the first to speak to the Porter. Who
indeed should it be if not this future traitor, of whom it might be
said, as of an equivocator, that he "committed treason enough
for God's sake, yet could not equivocate to heaven." It is no mere
chance that Macduff's companion in this scene is another traitor,
Lennox, who will convey the news to Macbeth that "Macduff is
fled to England" (IV, i).

It is difficult to say when Shakespeare conceived the idea of
including this scene in the play; the general opinion is that the
Porter's monologue was a later addition, creating what amounts

to a break in the action of the drama. One might venture a guess that these lines were composed when doubts about the character of Macduff arose in the mind of the author, and when the device of playing with allusion was woven into the texture of the play. Taken alone, any one of the episodes that I have analyzed would be inconclusive, but together they create a picture which does not correspond to the usual interpretation of Macduff as a positive hero. The new picture is rather appalling. The good are murdered (Duncan, Lady Macduff); the villains who kill them are themselves crushed (Macbeth and his wife); the archvillain lets the villain destroy the good, then destroys the villain and assumes the role of the good. All joust to win the leading roles in the cast of life.

In the course of their dialogue, the characters of Malcolm and Macduff acquire a new reflective consciousness; the action is momentarily interrupted as they take each other's measure. The masks and disguises handed down from the oldest theatrical tradition are now become flesh and blood, part of the characters' identity. The king is an actor. The extent to which this identification is linked to the transition of power in England is shown in *Measure for Measure,* which appeared in 1604, a year after the death of Queen Elizabeth. The play is interlaced with allusions to contemporary conditions, but sufficiently altered to avoid giving offense. The new leader, in the person of Angelo, appears to be nefarious, but the duke, who disguises himself as a monk and keeps watch from the shadows, returns to set everything right. This was perhaps what Shakespeare's contemporaries expected; but such hopes could be satisfied only in the realm of fable. Where does lost sovereignty end? On some remote island, and one must travel to the end of Prospero's world in *The Tempest* to rediscover it. The shipwreck, the terrifying opening scene, is the destruction of royal hopes; the tragedy is conveyed in a few lines, in a cry of horror and in silence. For the action to continue, the setting must be transposed to myth. This solution implies an altered awareness of sovereignty.

After the revelation of *Macbeth*, and Ulysses' speech in *Troilus and Cressida,* which we have defined as a well-spoken lie, there are two other decisive ideological moments in Shakespeare's theater. The first is Menenius Agrippa's apologue in *Coriolanus*. Near the beginning of the play, (I, i, 100ff.), Menenius, a reincarnation of Polonius, explains to the mutinous citizens the function of the senate-belly, inventing the famous tale of the body's members. He is listened to with understandable impatience; the speech is a parodic distortion of Ulysses' florid eloquence. Here the concept of social harmony is supported by a lie ill-spoken and is patently absurd. This speech is but a step to the second instance, represented by the rage in *Timon of Athens*. In the protagonist's desperate monologues, the social harmony that justifies power is ultimately revealed as substantial inharmony camouflaged by virtuous appearance: "for there is boundless theft / In limited professions." Further, Timon says to the bandits:

> Yet thanks I must you con
> That you are thieves profess'd, that you work not
> In holier shapes.
> [IV, iii, 431-433]

Here, with unmistakable precision, is what Macduff's son had intuited. The universal social larceny is but a reflection of the natural cosmic inharmony. Timon says:

> I'll example you with thievery:
> The sun's a thief, and with his great attraction
> Robs the vast sea: the moon's an arrant thief,
> And her pale fire she snatches from the sun.
> The sea's a thief, whose liquid surge resolves
> The moon into salt tears: the earth's a thief,
> That feeds and breeds by a composture stol'n
> From general excrement: each thing's a thief:
> The laws, your curb and whip, in their rough power
> Has unchecked theft.
> [IV, iii, 441-450]

157

Only in his late works does Shakespeare attempt to move beyond this extreme conception and toward an ideal of timeless harmony. This attempt involves a re-examination of the very concept of life, and is increasingly represented as an allegorical function of a mysterious justice which is cadenced by the "music of the spheres" announcing the happy ending of *Pericles;* by Ariel's song accompanying his prodigies as a sprite in *The Tempest;* by the secret music ending *Cymbeline* and *Henry VIII;* and by the music awaking Hermione from her statue-like sleep in *The Winter's Tale.* We are now well beyond *Macbeth,* on a horizon that calls for fresh explorations, new explorers.

As for Macbeth, with his mind "full of scorpions," he is a lion incapable of transforming himself into a fox, and is propelled toward a death he accepts as a deliverance. His monologue after Lady Macbeth's death would not be accepted by his enemies: for the victors, the world regains meaning. Only in defeat is life seen for what it is; but the cry of anguish is proof of nothing but defeat itself. This is perhaps true of life as well as of art. Thus *The Prince* would appear to be an *ars poetica* helping to define a world where pure sentiments are annihilated like innocent victims, where excessive ambition is mere folly, and where artifice and cunning conquer, leaving their audiences bewitched. Is he who rules by the word perhaps he who has penetrated most deeply into reality? Are the words of Timon to be trusted?

> . . . all is oblique;
> There's nothing level in our cursed natures
> But direct villainy.
>
> [IV, iii, 18–20]

6

Literary Models and the Autobiography of the Work

If one wishes to define the constant characteristics of the autobiography of the work, one can reduce them to two: the need to intervene obliquely in the work and the tendency to react to a literary model. As a consequence of the first of these, we must approach the explicit poetics of the work with caution. Modern criticism sprang from the perception of the work of art as a system to be deciphered, like the book of nature. If the key to this system were in the hands of the author, it would no longer be possible to speak of the work as an independent organism, for it would be a closed mechanism, controllable and definable by its creator. The characteristic of an organism, in contrast to a mechanism, is that it imposes law rather than conforming to it.

An explicit poetics, however, does not exhaust all the possibilities of aesthetic self-reflection. It is impossible to control a living organism: if the attempt is made with a human being, the reaction will be revolt, sometimes under the guise of neurosis. The same is true for any living thing or for a work of art; it is not possible to contravene their requirements without provoking a resistance which may go as far as a refusal to develop. Such is the case of a work *manqué,* which generally is a work that has been crushed by an authoritarian poetics.

The myth of genius, which today is often actively condemned, might be reevaluated if the artist were regarded as merely analogous to a gardener. Genius is in the work; the author need only have patience and confidence in his function as intermediary. This truth, openly acknowledged by Goethe, Coleridge, and Thomas Mann, was already operating in Homer, Dante, and Shakespeare. They all considered the work of art a phenomenon endowed with an autonomous existence. The book seems to be immobile, the picture unalterable, the architectural monument only susceptible to ruin. But in fact the works that have drawn life from an artist have remained alive, unlike their author who, if he somehow has survived, owes it to his creations.

If the work is an organism, it evolves and matures, at times revealing this process in the visible fabric but more often showing only the outcome of its growth. When the moment of artistic self-reflection arrives, the general tendency is to represent the conflict in a symbolic and oblique way. This is a phenomenon that pertains to all Western literature, from Homer to Joyce; a declared poetics does not seem to be the key to the work. The hidden key must be sought in the cells, in the knots of the text; just as an organism encloses its secret in the connective tissues of its being rather than in its beauty or its usefulness.

When it does find itself, the work leaves a mark, like a signal, on the page. And it is precisely here that the importance of the relation to the "literary model" is fully manifested. The most intense moments of self-reflection in the *Odyssey* arise from some recollection of the earlier Homeric poem; this occurs chiefly in the "Telemachy," the section of the *Odyssey* most resonant in this respect, permeated as it is with echoes and phantoms from the world of the *Iliad.* Dante's *Commedia* finds its point of departure in a dramatic comparison with the epic models of antiquity, directly in the case of the *Aeneid,* indirectly in that of the Homeric material, which reached Dante by the circuitous route of medieval translations into the vernacular. In Shakespeare's *Macbeth,* that key work of the artist's maturity, a complex process of reference and modification is effected, reinterpreting the Holinshed chronicle in the light of a Machiavellian meditation on the pregnant themes of power and destiny. In the *Iliad*, however, whose sources are buried in the oral tradition, we are confronted with an exception. Because of its total lack of reference to a prior work, it stands as the authentic first book; its principal passage of autobiography of the work, the description of Achilleus' shield, constitutes a comparison with an extraliterary art, that of figurative decoration.

If the relation to a literary model, or models, is so constant an element in the Western tradition, how, one may ask, has this influenced the relation of the work of art to reality? The question has engaged artists and theoreticians from antiquity to the present day. In general, the countless attempts to find an answer can be reduced to two identifiable categories: those theories which have recommended to the artist the imitation of a preexisting model, and those which have insisted on the necessity of imitating nature and its processes.

It is true, of course, that such a clear distinction cannot always be discerned; the Renaissance, for instance, was a period of intense debate about the two directions, with many artists following both tendencies. Yet the principal merit of the discussions (notably frequent after the inception of Romanticism) has been a defining of the actual limits of the problem. There is the literary or artistic tradition on the one hand (a model or congeries of models fixed in time), and the concept of a model of reality or of nature (the world and society), on the other; in short, the model taken from the life the artist sees before him and which he is called upon to portray. What, in relation to the two, is the work in progress—the new work, the future model still struggling to assert an identity not yet evident?

If the Western artistic tradition has always oscillated between the imitation of the artistic model and the imitation of reality, it is because European culture has been impelled to identify with archetypes (including artistic ones) and at the same time to break away from them. Roman Jakobson has found in this culture the presence of "two orders: the traditional canon and the artistic novelty as a deviation from that canon.... This simultaneous preservation of tradition and breaking away from tradition forms the essence of every new work of art." Something of a traumatic and at the same time liberating nature is established: the separation from the model, the abandonment of the guide. A deep oedipal relationship unfolds at the heart of Western literature which, not without reason, is proficient in obliquity and sublimation. Before he has achieved his own originality, the artist experiences the literary tradition as a love-hate relationship, as is shown in one of the subtlest instances of the autobiography of the work: the opening chapters of *Don Quixote* by Cervantes.

The equivalence of the *hidalgo* and the author is made explicit in the first chapter: ". . . many a time he was tempted to take up his pen and literally finish the tale as had been promised, and he undoubtedly would have done so, and would have succeeded at it very well, if his thoughts had not been constantly occupied with other things of greater moment" (*Portable Cervantes*, p. 59).

Don Quixote is also the author at the beginning of his work. The chivalric literature that obsesses him is the same as that which fascinates Cervantes, and the protagonist enters the world in the same way as the writer embarks on a novel. This is the reason why great importance is given to the names of the characters in these first chapters. The difficulty of finding the appropriate names denotes the effort of detaching oneself from a literature in which the identity of the characters has been unquestioned, the correct names always coming to the author's mind as a matter of course. But what would be the proper spelling of Don Quixote? And how is Don Quixote going to name his horse, and his lady? The reader may recall the lengthy discussion devoted to these problems by the protagonist. Cervantes, the modern novelist, is aware of the arbitrary nature of the fictional character and secretly envies the situation of the epic, with its well-established names and identities.

Don Quixote is obsessed with the desire to be a consecrated knight—of necessity, on the basis of other men's deeds, since he himself has done nothing. The situation is tantamount to that of a writer who wants recognition for an originality not yet achieved. At the beginning of Part II of the book Don Quixote and Sancho Panza will talk about themselves as of characters already existing in a novel. But in Part I, Don Quixote-Cervantes is the protagonist-author of a book still to be written: the whiteness of the arms symbolizes blank pages; the shield without insignia, work still to be done.

At the outset of his journey the protagonist recites a lyrical soliloquy derived from the tradition that has impelled him to action, and Cervantes observes that in fact he is treading the very ground that he is celebrating in literary terms. Don Quixote stands between a fiction to be imitated and a reality to be transformed into a new fiction. "And so he went on, stringing together absurdities, all of a kind that his books had taught him, imitating insofar as he was able the language of their authors" (p. 66).

The confrontation with reality takes place in the first inn described by Cervantes. Here again we witness the conflict between the literary tradition and reality. Don Quixote continues to employ his own precious language in spite of the pressing problem of naming the things of the world. The fish that is served to the *hidalgo* is called *abadejo* in Castille, *bacallao* in Andalusia, and *curadillo* or *truchuella* elsewhere. From characters to things, all await a definitive baptism. It is, however, significant that Don Quixote asks the innkeeper to consecrate him as a knight; by so doing the innkeeper also consecrates Cervantes as a writer, which suggests that the world of taverns, merchants, brigands, beggars, and *picaros* will establish his originality, while the world of knights, princes, and their ladies, often presented nostalgically in the novel, will have only the shadowy lineaments of a dream.

In Chapter IV, after his investiture as a knight, Don Quixote meets with two adventures. His attempt to protect Andrea from his master's beating exemplifies the impracticality of applying the heroic code to reality, a constant theme throughout the novel. But more important for our purpose is the meeting with the merchants. Don Quixote tries to extract from them a commendation of Dulcinea's beauty, which they are willing to give, if only to be rid of this outlandish nuisance; but first they demand to see her portrait. The merchants represent a significant part of the audience that Cervantes is addressing, a public prepared to believe the impossible, but only on its own terms. This inaugurates the poetics of the bourgeois romance based on a covenant: give us reality and we will believe your fable.

Don Quixote's first entrance into the world demonstrates that it is impossible for a writer to explore reality without first revising his relationship to literary models. This is the function of the *escrutinio* of the books conducted by the priest and the barber. Don Quixote's library is sealed, but the two friends fail to dissuade the *hidalgo* from his enterprise. As the "figure" of a writer, the protagonist understands that the two worlds, the chivalric tradition on the one hand and everyday life on the other, are incomplete: both are inadequate in themselves to support a work of originality. At this point Cervantes accepts the division between the two worlds and decides to use it as the basis of his novel. The creation of the character of Sancho Panza is the decisive stroke for the identity of the work. The bourgeois novel, with its nostalgia for the heroic and its fascination with reality, is born. Its first expression is seen in Don Quixote's assault on the windmills.

At the end of Chapter VIII, Cervantes leaves his hero arm in air, poised for a duel, the outcome of which the author is unable to find in the chronicles he has consulted. In the next chapter we have the invention of the manuscript written by Cide Hamete Benengeli. This imaginary text fills the void left by the collapse of the chivalric tradition, giving the writer the assurance that he is moving in a world which has already been described. From this point on, he will be a "translator" rather than a writer; but the device of the manuscript is above all linked to the intuition that the author is dependent on the work, and not vice versa. The author who "translates" has the feeling that the work has in some way already been written, just as Michelangelo felt that the statue was already present in the marble, waiting only for the artist to free it. The itinerary of the autobiography of the work, which runs through the first chapters of *Don Quixote,* finds its culmination in its author's acceptance of the function of intermediary, or "translator." As when Dante meets Beatrice, when Cervantes finds his way, he performs an act of submission. The ritual is highly ironic in that the author of the original text is an Arab, who, as Cervantes suggests, may well be a liar. The substance of the ritual is nonetheless serious: from this moment on the author-translator will defer to the work and conform to its needs. *Don Quixote,* with its double author, becomes a work with a double protagonist, addressed to a double audience of noblemen and merchants.

Thus the autobiography of the work marks the separation from the model and the approach to a reality that the artist recognizes as his own. Shakespeare in *Macbeth* showed that it is not always necessary that the model to be replaced be a work of literary genius: in the nineteenth century, Dostoyevsky found in the serial novels of the period a model to be overthrown. Between Shakespeare and the authorized historiographers of various epochs, there was always, from Plutarch to Holinshed, a dependent-resistant relationship. As sources of inspiration, they provided him with innumerable themes, characters, and situations. The manifold human pageant they present to the reader was perceived by Shakespeare with a combination of fascination and exasperation, which infiltrated many of the tragedies and historical dramas in isolated comments of plebeians, monologues of problematical protagonists, and a blazing amalgam of comedy and tragedy characteristic of his theater. The autobiography of the work is not confined to *Macbeth;* it runs through all of Shakespeare's work, from *Romeo and Juliet* to *Hamlet,* and the late plays such as *Cymbeline* and *The Tempest.* To have singled out *Macbeth* is to have selected a particularly sensitive moment in the evolution of this work in continual progress, when the reading of the Bible and Seneca and the discovery of Machiavelli led the writer to an understanding of the apocalyptic cruelty of reality and of the interchangeability of human roles. Macbeth's great monologue on the death of Lady Macbeth, this crown of his artistic maturity and final discovery of his own reality, would not have been possible without the subtle and crucial colloquy between Macduff and Malcolm with its implication of the abandonment of a faith in the legitimacy of power, a faith which pervades the historiography that Shakespeare used as a model.

The need for a literary model, for its "paternal" function, is underlined by the fact that without it, there would be no possibility of looking at the world as material for artistic endeavor. The model (and the literary tradition it evokes) is like the grammar and syntax of the poetic representation; without a model a writer would be incapable of "reading" reality. Thus it teaches him, in a literary sense, to read the world as a text to be reordered and recomposed. From this standpoint, it would be difficult to overestimate the importance of the literary tradition that lies behind every artist.

Still more important is the representation of the world, the attempt to create a new grammar and a new syntax. If the encounter with reality fails, the writer's effort is reduced to an acceptance of the model—imitation, mannerism—or to an entirely conventional opposition, a programmatic reversal at the expressive level in which the literary tradition is desanctified in a parodic way, but paradoxically reaffirmed as the model. Liberation from the model does not occur at the literary level but at the level of confrontation with reality.

The work of art is a discourse with the world which tactically utilizes dialogue together with other literary forms. This affirmation may not find favor in the present period of critical methodology which, in its variety, presents one constant element: the tendency to view the work from an exclusively literary perspective, and thus to make the relation between art and reality parenthetical. Yet the capacity of a work to create a Weltanschauung is the touchstone of its originality. When our culture recovers this conviction, it will be clear that in the methodological-critical attitude of recent years the various interpreters have expressed a gnosiological crisis, which has influenced the whole of contemporary literary debate. Eventually we will return to the cognitive value of the work of art, to literature as an instrument for the interpretation of reality.

My vision of the literary achievement is based on the conviction that the function of art is to represent the *other than itself* with all the risks and difficulties this entails. Only the encounter with reality renders art not merely possible but necessary; without it the literary experience is reduced to a dialogue among critics and the proponents of the various hermeneutic tendencies. The interpreters must also seek the world in books; this is perhaps the means of gauging the depth of what they read.

Bibliography

Introduction

Abrams, Meyer H. *The Mirror and the Lamp.* New York, 1958. (Esp. chs. 7 and 8.)

Booth, Wayne. *The Rhetoric of Fiction.* Chicago, 1973.

Brooks, Cleanth. "The Poem as an Organism." *English Institute Annual,* 1940, pp. 20-41.

_____. "Implications of an Organic Theory of Poetry." *Literature and Belief,* ed. M. H. Abrams. English Institute Essays. New York, 1958.

Carlyle, Thomas. "The Hero as Poet." In: *On Heroes, Hero-Worship and the Heroic in History.* London, 1840.

Coleridge, Samuel. *Biographia Literaria,* ed. J. Shawcross. Oxford, 1907.

_____. *Theory of Life.* In: *The Complete Works of S. T. Coleridge.* 7 vols. New York, 1854. Vol. 1.

Heidegger, Martin. *Poetry, Language, Thought,* transl. A. Hofstadter. New York, 1972.

Montale, Eugenio. *Nel Nostro Tempo.* Milan, 1972 (the translation of the quoted passage is mine).

Schopenhauer, Arthur. *The World as Will and Representation,* transl. E. F. J. Payne. New York, 1969.

Shelley, Percy B. *Defence of Poetry.* In: *Shelley's Literary and Philosophical Criticism,* ed. J. Shawcross. Oxford, 1909.

Homer

Adorno, Theodor W. *Dialectics of Enlightenment,* transl. J. Cumming. New York, 1972.

Amory, Anne. "The Gates of Horn and Ivory." *Yale Classical Studies,* 20 (1966), 1–58.

Arrowsmith, William A. "Helen on the Walls." *Hudson Review,* 15 (1962), 567–570.

Auerbach, Erich. *Mimesis.* Princeton, 1953.

Berard, Victor. *Did Homer Live?,* transl. Brian Rhys. London and Toronto, 1931.

———. *Les Navigations d'Ulysse.* Paris, 1927–1929.

Bespaloff, Rachel. *On the Iliad,* transl. Mary McCarthy. New York, 1948.

Bowra, Cecil M. *Homer.* New York, 1972.

———. *Tradition and Design in the Iliad.* Oxford, 1930.

Campbell, Joseph. *The Hero with a Thousand Faces.* New York, 1951.

Dimock, George E., Jr. "The Name of Odysseus." *Hudson Review,* 9 (1956), 52–70.

Dodds, Eric. *The Greeks and the Irrational.* Cambridge, Mass., 1960.

Else, Gerard F. *Homer and the Homeric Problem.* Cincinnati, 1965.

Fagles, Robert. "Homer and the Writers." In: *Homer: A Collection of Critical Essays,* ed. George Steiner and Robert Fagles. Englewood Cliffs, N.J., 1962.

Germain, G. *Genèse de l'Odyssée.* Paris, 1954.

Guthrie, William K. C. *The Greeks and Their Gods.* Boston, 1950.

Havelock, Eric A. *Preface to Plato.* Cambridge, Mass., 1963.

———. *Prologue to Greek Literacy.* Cincinnati, 1971.

Jaeger, Werner. *Paideia: The Ideals of Greek Culture,* transl. Gilbert Highet. New York, 1939.

Kirk, Geoffrey. *The Songs of Homer.* Cambridge, 1962.

Lord, Albert. *The Singer of Tales.* Cambridge, Mass., 1960.

Mansfield, J. "Heraclitus on the Psychology of Sleep and on the Rivers." *Mnemosyne,* 20 (1967), 1–29.

Mazon, Paul. *Introduction à l'Iliade.* Paris, 1958.

Mireaux, E. *Les poèmes Homériques et l'histoire Grècque.* Paris 1948–1949.

Myres, John. *Homer and His Critics.* London, 1958.

Nagler, Michael. *Spontaneity and Tradition: A Study in the Oral Art of Homer.* Berkeley, 1974.

Night, J. W. F. *Many-Minded Homer,* ed. J. C. Christie. New York, 1968.

Otto, Walter. *The Homeric Gods,* transl. Moses Hadas. New York, 1954.

Page, Denys. *History and the Homeric Iliad.* Berkeley, 1959.

———. *The Homeric Odyssey.* Oxford, 1955.

Parry, Milman. *The Making of Homeric Verse.* Oxford, 1971.

Rieu, Emile. *The Odyssey.* London, 1946.

Scott, John. *The Unity of Homer.* Berkeley, 1921.

Snell, Bruno. *The Discovery of the Mind,* transl. T. G. Rosenmeyer. Cambridge, Mass., 1953.

Stanford, W. B. *The Ulysses Theme: A Study in the Adaptability of a Traditional Hero.* Oxford, 1954.

Stawell, Florence. *Homer and the Iliad.* London, 1909.

Steiner, George. "Homer and the Scholars." In: *Homer: A Collection of Critical Essays,* ed. George Steiner and Robert Fagles. Englewood, N.J., 1962.

Taylor, Charles, Jr. "The Obstacles to Odysseus' Return." *Yale Review,* 50 (1961), 569–580.

Thomson, James A. *Studies in the Odyssey.* Oxford, 1914.

Weil, Simone. *The Iliad, or the Poem of Force.* Wallingford, Pa., 1948.

Whitman, Cedric H. *Homer and the Heroic Tradition.* Cambridge, Mass., 1958.

Woodhouse, William J. *The Composition of Homer's Odyssey.* Oxford, 1930.

Dante

Auerbach, Eric. *Dante, Poet of the Secular World,* transl. R. Mannheim. Chicago, 1961.

——. "Figura." *Archivium Romanicum,* 22 (1938), 436–489.

Barbi, Michele. *Problemi fondamentali per un nuovo commento della Divina Commedia.* Florence, 1955 (esp. ch.: "Allegoria e lettera nella Divina Commedia").

Batard, Yvonne. *Dante, Minerve et Apollon.* Paris, 1951. (Esp. ch.: "Image 'pure' ou Apollon sans Minerve: Gérion.")

Boccaccio, Giovanni. *Il Comento sopra la Commedia.* Florence, 1863, Vol. 1, ch. 1.

Comparetti, Domenico. *Vergil in the Middle Ages,* transl. F. M. Benecke. Hamden, Conn., 1966.

Consoli, D. *Significato del Virgilio dantesco.* Florence, 1967.

Curtius, Ernst R. *European Literature and the Latin Middle Ages,* transl. W. R. Trask. New York, 1953.

De Bruyne, E. *The Esthetics of the Middle Ages,* transl. E. B. Hennessy. New York, 1969.

Della Terza, Dante. "Medieval Poetics and Contemporary Audiences." *Medievalia and Humanistica,* 7 (1976).

D'Ovidio, Francesco. *Studi sulla Divina Comedia.* Milan, 1901. (Esp. ch.: "L'Epistola a Cangrande.")

BIBLIOGRAPHY

Eliot, T. S. *Dante*. London, 1929.

Fletcher, Angus. *Allegory: The Theory of a Symbolic Mode*. Ithaca, N.Y., 1964.

Fraser, A. *The War against Poetry*. Princeton, 1970.

Freccero, John. "A Letter to the Author." In: Harold Bloom, *The Anxiety of Influence*. New York, 1973. Pp. 122–123 (on Beatrice's apparition to Dante).

Gilbert, Allen. "Did Dante Dedicate the *Paradise* to Cangrande della Scala?." *Italica*, 43 (1966), 100–124.

Greene, Richard. "Dante's Allegory of the Poets and the Medieval Theory of Poetic Fiction." *Comparative Literature*, 9 (1957), 118–128.

Hallock, Ann H. "Dante's *Selva Oscura* and Other Obscure *Selvas*." *Forum Italicum*, 6 (1973), 57–78.

Hardie, C. "The Epistle to Cangrande Again." *Deutsches Dante-Jahrbuch*, 38 (1960), 51–64.

Huizinga, Johan. *The Waning of the Middle Ages*. New York, 1924. (Esp. ch.: "Symbolism in Its Decline".)

Ladner, G. B. "Vegetation Symbolism and the Concept of Renaissance." *Essays in Honor of Erwin Panofsky*. Vol. 1. New York, 1961.

Lanapoppi, Aleramo. "*La Divina Commedia:* allegoria 'dei poeti' to allegoria 'dei teologi'?" *Dante Studies*, 86 (1968), 17–39.

Lewis, Clive S. *The Allegory of Love: A Study in Medieval Tradition*. Oxford, 1936.

Logan, Terence. "The Characterization of Ulysses in Homer, Virgil and Dante: A Study in Sources and Analogues." *82nd Annual Report of the Dante Society*, 1964, pp. 19–46.

Mazzeo, Joseph A. *Medieval Cultural Tradition in Dante's Comedy*. Ithaca, N.Y., 1960.

Mazzoni, Francesco. "L'Epistola a Cangrande." *Rendiconti del'Accademia nazionale dei Lincei*, 10:3–4 (1955), 157–198.

Moore, Edward. *Studies in Dante, First Series: Scripture and Classical Authors in Dante*. Oxford, 1896 (repr. 1969).

Nardi, Bruno. *Dal "Convivio" alla "Commedia."* Rome, 1960.

————. *Lectura Dantis Scaligera: Il punto sull'epistola a Cangrande*. Florence, 1960.

Padoan, Giorgio. *Il pio Enea, l'empio Ulisse*. Ravenna, 1977.

Porena, Manfredi. "Il titolo della *Divina Commedia*." *Rendiconti dell'Accademia nazionale dei Lincei*, 6: 1–4 (1933), 114–141.

Rajna, Pio. "Il titolo del poema dantesco." *Studi Danteschi*, 4 (1921), 5–37.

Renaudet, Augustin. *Dante humaniste*. Paris, 1952.

Renucci, Paul. *Dante, disciple et juge du monde gréco-latin*. Paris, 1954.

Scott, J. A. "Inferno XXVI: Dante's Ulysses," *Lettere Italiane*, 23 (1971), 145-186.

Singleton, Charles. *Dante Studies I: Commedia: Elements of Structure.* Cambridge, Mass., 1954.

_____. *Dante Studies II: Journey to Beatrice.* Cambridge, Mass., 1958.

Steiner, George. "Dante Now: The Gossip of Eternity." In: *On Difficulty and Other Essays.* New York and Oxford, 1978.

Thompson, David. *Dante's Epic Journey.* Baltimore, 1974.

Vossler, Karl. *Medieval Culture*, transl. W. C. Lawton. New York, 1929.

Whitfield, John. *Dante and Vergil.* Oxford, 1949.

Shakespeare

Abel, Lionel. *Metatheatre.* New York, 1963.

Allen, Michael. "Macbeth's Genial Porter." *English Literary Renaissance,* 4 (1974), 326-336.

Bartholemeusz, Dennis. *Macbeth and the Players.* Cambridge, 1969.

Biggins, D. "Sexuality, Witchcraft and Violence in *Macbeth.*" *Shakespeare Studies,* 8 (1975), 255-277.

Bradbrook, M. C. "The Sources of *Macbeth.*" *Shakespeare Survey,* 4 (1951), 35-48.

Braddock, Muriel. *Elizabethan Stage Conditions,* Hamden, Conn., 1932 (repr. 1962).

Bradley, Andrew. *Shakespearean Tragedy.* London, 1904 (repr. 1960).

Brooks, Cleanth. *The Well Wrought Urn.* New York, 1947. (Ch.: "The Naked Babe and the Clock of Manliness".)

Burrel, M. G. *Macbeth:* A Study in Paradox." *Shakespeare Jahrbuch,* 90 (1954), 167-190.

Curry, Walter. *Shakespeare's Philosophical Patterns,* Baton Rouge, 1937.

Duthie, G. I. "Shakespeare's *Macbeth:* A Study in Tragic Absurdity." *English Studies Today,* 318 (1961), 121-128.

Elliott, George. *Dramatic Providence in Macbeth.* Princeton, 1960.

Farnham, Willard. *Shakespeare's Tragic Frontier.* Berkeley, 1950.

Fergusson, Francis. "*Macbeth* as an Imitation of an Action." *English Institute Essays,* ed. A. S. Downer. New York, 1952.

Freud, Sigmund. "Some Character-Types Met with in Psycho-Analytical Work." In: *Macbeth: A Selection of Critical Essays,* ed. J. Wain. London, 1968.

Frye, Northrop. *Fools of Time: Studies in Shakespearean Tragedy.* Toronto, 1967.

Harcourt, John. "I Pray You, Remember the Porter." *Shakespeare Quarterly*, 12 (1961), 393–402.

Hawkes, Terence. *Shakespeare and the Reason*. Cambridge, 1969.

Heilman, Robert. "The Criminal as Tragic Hero." *Shakespeare Survey*, 19 (1966), 12–24.

Iwasaki, Soji. *The Sword and the Word: Shakespeare's Tragic Sense of Time*. Tokyo, 1973.

Jorgensen, Paul. *Our Naked Frailties: Sensational Art and Meaning in Macbeth*. Los Angeles-Berkeley, 1971.

Kantak, V. Y. "An Approach to Shakespearean Tragedy: The 'Actor' Image in *Macbeth*." *Shakespeare Survey*, 16 (1963), 42–52.

Kleinstuck, J. "Ulysses' Speech on Degree as Related to the Play of *Troilus and Cressida*." *Neophilologus*, 43 (1959), 58–63.

Knight, George Wilson. *The Imperial Theme*. London, 1931 (repr. 1954).

———. *The Wheel of Fire*. London, 1930 (repr. 1962).

Knights, Lionel C. *Some Shakespearean Themes*. London, 1959.

Lawrence, William. *The Elizabethan Playhouse and Other Studies*. New York, 1963.

Levin, Harry. *The Question of Hamlet*. New York, 1959.

———. *Shakespeare and the Revolution of the Times: Perspectives and Commentaries*. Cambridge, Mass., 1976.

McGee, A. R. "*Macbeth* and the Furies." *Shakespeare Survey*, 19 (1966), 55–67.

Mack, Maynard, Jr. *Killing the King: Three Studies in Shakespeare's Tragic Structure*. New Haven, Conn., 1973.

Mahood, Molly. *Shakespeare's Word Play*. London, 1957.

Markels, Julian. "The Spectacle of Deterioration: *Macbeth* and the 'Manner' of Tragic Imitation." *Shakespeare Quarterly*, 12 (1961), 293–303.

Muir, Kenneth, "Image and Symbol in *Macbeth*." *Shakespeare Survey*, 19 (1966), 45–54.

———. *Shakespeare's Tragic Sequence*. London, 1972.

Murry, J. M. *Shakespeare*. London, 1935.

Pack, Robert. "*Macbeth:* The Anatomy of Loss." *Yale Review*, 45 (1956), 533–548.

Paul, Henry N. *The Royal Play of Macbeth*. New York, 1949 (repr. 1971).

Praz, Mario. *Machiavelli and the Elizabethans*. Folcroft, Pa., 1928 (repr. 1970).

Quinones, Ricardo. *The Renaissance Discovery of Time*. Cambridge, Mass., 1973.

Raab, Felix. *The English Face of Machiavelli*. London, 1964.

Righter, Ann. *Shakespeare and the Idea of the Play*. London, 1962.

174

Rossiter, Arthur. *Angels with Horns.* London, 1961.

Schucking, Levin. *The Baroque Character of the Elizabethan Tragic Hero.* New York, 1949.

Sears, Lloyd. *Shakespeare's Philosophy of Evil.* North Quincy, Mass., 1974.

Shakespeare's Holinshed: The Chronicle and the Historical Plays compared by W. G. Boswell-Stone. London, 1896 (repr. 1907).

Spencer, Theodore. *Shakespeare and the Nature of Man.* New York, 1942 (repr. 1961).

Spurgeon, Caroline. *Shakespeare's Imagery and What It Tells Us.* Cambridge, 1935 (repr. 1969).

Stoll, Elmer. *Shakespearean Studies.* New York, 1942 (repr. 1960).

Valesio, Paolo. "'That glib and oylie art': Cordelia and the Rhetoric of Antirhetoric." *Versus: Quaderno di Studi Semiotici,* 16/5 (1977), 91–117.

Walker, Roy. *The Time Is Free: A Study of Macbeth.* London, 1949.

Weitz, Morris. *Hamlet and the Philosophy of Literary Criticism.* Chicago, 1964.

Wickham, Glynne. "Hell-Castle and Its Door-Keeper." *Shakespeare Survey,* 19 (1966), 68–74.

Literary Models

Cervantes, Miguel de. *Don Quixote.* In: *The Portable Cervantes,* transl. and ed. S. Putnam. New York, 1951.

Foucault, Michel. *Les Mots et les choses.* Paris, 1966 (on Cervantes: pp. 60 ff.).

Frye, Northrop. *Fables of Identity: Studies in Poetic Mythology.* New York, 1963.

Gombrich, Ernst H. *Art and Illusion: A Study in the Psychology of Pictorial Representation.* Princeton, 1961.

Graff, Gerald. *Literature against Itself.* Chicago, 1979.

Jakobson, Roman. "The Dominant." In: *Readings in Russian Poetics,* ed. L. Matejka and K. Pomorska. Cambridge, Mass., 1971.

Robert, Marthe. *L'Ancien et le nouveau.* Paris, 1963.

Index

Argonauts, 56
Aristotle, 64
Arnaut Daniel, 118
Autobiography of the work, 12, 17, 30, 34–35, 60–62, 83, 103, 159, 162, 165

Benvenuto da Imola, 100
Boccaccio, Giovanni, 19, 100, 149
Bonagiunta da Lucca, 95, 117, 119
Booth, Wayne, 15
Brooks, Cleanth, 12
Brunetto Latini, 96

Camus, Albert, 19
Carlyle, Thomas, 12
Cavalcanti, Guido, 85, 86
Cervantes, Miguel de, 162–165
Ciardi, John, 86
Coleridge, Samuel, 12, 160, 169
Curtius, Ernst R., 66

Dante, 11, 12, 13, 66–102, 103–124, 160, 165; Convivio, 13, 83; De Vulgari Eloquentia, 80, 81; Letter to Can Grande, 13, 66, 78, 81, 100–102

Defoe, Daniel, 19
Diderot, Denis, 137
Donne, John, 134

Elizabeth (Queen), 133, 156

Ferrers, A. G., 81
Forese Donati, 95, 117, 118
Freud, Sigmund, 19, 131–132, 173

Giacomino da Verona, 96
Goethe, Wolfgang, 12, 160
Guinizzelli, Guido, 95, 118, 119

Heidegger, Martin, 13
Herder, Johann Gottfried, 12
Holinshed, Raphael, 129, 144, 147, 149
Homer, 11, 12, 16, 17–65, 77, 96, 104, 105–106, 160, 169; Iliad, 17–33; Odyssey, 34–65; Siege and return as narrative archetypes in, 17–19, 44–45, 54–56, 64–65; "Telemachy," 34–40
Horace, 95, 101–102

177

INDEX

Jakobson, Roman, 161-162
James (King), 16, 129-136, 144
Joyce, James, 15

Knight, G. Wilson, 135

Lucan, 95
Lucretius, 19

Machiavelli, Niccolò, 139-140, 141,
    142, 149, 150, 158, 165
Mann, Thomas, 160
Manzoni, Alessandro, 19
Michelangelo, 164-165
Montale, Eugenio, 14-15
Muir, Kenneth, 145

Old Testament, 20, 78, 165
Organism (art as), 12-13, 15, 63-64
    123-124, 160
Ovid, 95

Paul, Henry, N., 130
Paul, Saint, 79, 80
Pier delle Vigne, 112-114, 123
Pirandello, Luigi, 14
Plato, 80, 96
Pound, Ezra, 124

Proteus (myth of), 11, 34
Ptolomeus, 140

Schopenhauer, Arthur, 12-13
Seneca, 165
Shakespeare, William, 11, 12, 16,
    125-158, 160, 165-166; *Hamlet*,
    13, 132-135, 140, 143, 150, 165;
    Julius Caesar, 133; *King Lear*, 133,
    135, 144; *Macbeth*, 11, 16, 125-
    158, 165; *Richard III*, 142, 143,
    150; *The Tempest*, 156, 158, 165;
    Timon of Athens, 132, 134, 157,
    158; *Troilus and Cressida*, 140, 156
Shelley, Percy B., 15
Singleton, Charles, 85
Sophocles, 20
Spencer, Theodore, 132
Statius, 95, 115-121

Toynbee, Paget, 80

Virgil, 71-124; *Aeneid*, 81, 82, 88, 90,
    92, 93, 111, 114

Waith, Eugene M., 145
Wilson, J. Dover, 145

Zola, Emile, 15

The Poetics of Disguise

Designed by Richard E. Rosenbaum.
Composed by The Composing Room of Michigan, Inc.
in 10 point Baskerville V.I.P., 3 points leaded,
with display lines in Baskerville.
Printed offset by Thomson/Shore, Inc. on
Warren's Number 66 Antique Offset, 50 pound basis.
Bound by John H. Dekker & Sons, Inc.
in Holliston book cloth
and stamped in All Purpose foil.

Library of Congress Cataloging in Publication Data

Ferrucci, Franco, 1936–
  The poetics of disguise.

  "Some of the material . . . was originally published in Italian in essay form; it has been thoroughly revised for the English version."
  Bibliography: p.
  Includes index.
  CONTENTS: The Shield of Achilleus.—The return of Odysseus.—The meeting with Geryon.—[etc.]
  1. Literature—History and criticism—Addresses, essays, lectures. 2. Homer—Criticism and interpretation—Addresses, essays, lectures. 3. Dante Alighieri, 1265–1321. Divina commedia—Addresses, essays, lectures. 4. Shakespeare, William, 1564–1616. Macbeth—Addresses, essays, lectures. I. Title.
PN511. f45 1980   809   80-11242
ISBN 0-8014-1262-5